Foreword to the Code of Practice on the Identification and Assessment of Special Educational Needs

This Foreword is not part of the Code of Practice.

fore the last date

Foreword

Introduction

1. The 1993 Education Act requires the Secretary of State to issue a Code of Practice giving practical guidance to local education authorities (LEAs) and the governing bodies of all maintained schools on their responsibilities towards all children with special educational needs (SEN). Those responsibilities are set out in Part III of the Act. It has been estimated that, nationally, some 20 per cent of the school population will have special educational needs at some time during their school career. The Code seeks to help schools and LEAs obtain best value from the considerable financial resources and expertise they devote to the education of children with special educational needs of various descriptions, from those who need a little extra help to those with more serious learning difficulties.

2. The Code of Practice on the Identification and Assessment of Special Educational Needs has been approved by Parliament. The text reflects extensive consultation with schools, LEAs, the health services, social services and voluntary agencies. The Code will come into effect on 1 September 1994. From that date, LEAs, schools and all those who help them work with children with special educational needs, including the health services and the social services, must have regard to the Code – see below.

3. This Foreword explains the status of the Code; highlights related developments such as monitoring arrangements, the publication of a Guide for Parents and the establishment of the SEN Tribunal; and describes the Regulations and Circulars which should be read alongside the Code. The Foreword is not formally part of the Code itself.

The status of the Code

4. Part III of the 1993 Education Act and Regulations made thereunder build upon the principles and practices first set out in the 1981 Act. They place duties and responsibilities on LEAs and schools, the health services and social services.

5. Those bodies must, of course, fulfil their duties. But it is up to them to decide how to do so, in the light of the guidance of the Code of Practice. Thus, for example, under the 1993 Act, as under the 1981 Act, maintained schools must use their best endeavours to make provision for pupils with special educational needs. The Code's guidance is designed to help schools make effective decisions. Similarly, local education authorities must, when necessary, make assessments and statements of children's special educational needs and do so within the statutory timescales. The Code offers guidance to LEAs as to the circumstances in which assessments and statements might be made. It does not – and could not – tell them what to do in each individual case.

E0004592759001

6. All those to whom the Code applies have a statutory duty to have regard to it; they must not ignore it. This means that, from 1 September 1994, whenever schools and LEAs decide what they should do for children with special educational needs, and whenever the health services and social services help schools and LEAs take action on behalf of such children, those bodies must consider what the Code says.

7. The duty to have regard to the Code begins on 1 September 1994 and will continue for the lifetime of the Code. But the effect of having regard to the Code may vary according to circumstances and over time. Thus, for example, schools' governing bodies and head teachers should reflect, in the light of the Code, on the way in which their schools identify, assess and make provision for children with special educational needs. In that way, they will be having regard to the Code. But the detail of what they decide to do may vary according to the size, organisation, location and pupil population of the school. The effect of their having regard to the Code is also likely to develop with time: much will depend upon schools' starting points. It would be unrealistic to expect all schools to have in place on 1 September 1994 procedures matching those set out in the Code's guidance. But it is reasonable to require all schools to have regard to the Code from that date and thereafter to plan their provision in the light of the Code.

8. These considerations are reflected in the Regulations governing the information that schools must publish. It is not practicable to expect all schools to have published information on their SEN policies on 1 September 1994. Many schools may be able to do so but some will need time to consider their policies in the light of the Code. The Regulations say that schools must publish information on their SEN policies by 1 August 1995, and must report to parents on the implementation of their policies in the first annual report published after that date and in all subsequent reports. Regulations will be introduced to provide that schools summarise their special educational needs policies in the prospectuses they publish in the autumn of 1995. Schools will, of course, wish to keep their policies and practices under review in the light of experience and having regard to the Code. Again, therefore, the effect of the Code can be expected to develop over time.

9. The Code recognises that there is a continuum of special educational needs and that such needs are found across the range of ability. The Code also recognises that the continuum of needs should be reflected in a continuum of provision.

10. The special educational needs of most children can be met effectively in mainstream schools, with outside specialist help if necessary, but without a statutory assessment or a statement. The Code recommends that, to help match special educational provision to children's needs, schools and LEAs should adopt a staged approach.

11. As guidance, the Code sets out a five-stage model. It stresses that stages are not an automatic progression towards, nor barriers in the way of, statements: they are means of matching provision to need. Moreover, they can and should be firmly embedded in the general work of the school. Thus, for example, stage 1 in the Code's model is characterised by the gathering of information and increased differentiation within the child's normal classroom work. Such special attention and help constitutes special educational provision as the term is used in the Act and the Code, and can be of significant benefit to the children who need it.

12. Stages 2 and 3 are characterised, respectively, by the creation of individual education plans and the involvement of outside specialists. In practice, the precise definition of the stages and the number of stages adopted are matters for schools and LEAs to decide, consulting each other, in the light of the Code. But OFSTED inspections will consider the effectiveness of schools' policies and practices for identifying, assessing and making provision for children's special educational needs, in the light of schools' policies and in the light of the Code.

13. Like schools, LEAs, the health services and social services must have regard to the Code from 1 September 1994. LEAs must observe the new Regulations, including the statutory time limits, whenever, after 1 September 1994, they begin to make an assessment. Statements made under the 1981 Act will be valid legal documents under the new system. But some transitional arrangements are necessary to ensure a smooth transition between the old and new regimes. These arrangements are set out in the Appendix to the Code. They seek to ensure a fair deal for both parents and LEAs. They accordingly fix 31 December 1994 as the end date for assessments made under the 1981 Act and, at the same time, ensure that LEAs will be able to adjust to the new regime.

Monitoring the Code

14. The operation of Part III of the 1993 Education Act, including the effect of the Code of Practice, will be closely monitored. Registered Inspectors will look closely at schools' SEN policies and practices in the light of the Code, taking into account the considerations in paragraphs 6–11 above. OFSTED and OHMCI (Wales), in their examination of and reports on the education system, will also monitor and evaluate the impact of the Code and other measures and will in the course of this work look, for example, at the impact of special educational needs support services. The Department for Education will review LEAs' implementation of the Act, including their performance against the new time limits for the making of assessments and statements.

15. The Secretary of State will consider, in the light of this evaluation, whether and when the Code should be revised. All those to whom the Code applies are likely to welcome a period of stability in which they can adapt their policies and practices. But the Code should also be a living document and should therefore be kept up-to-date in the light of experience. The Secretary of State will, of course, as the Act requires, consult upon any proposed revision and seek Parliament's approval for any new draft.

Partnership with parents

16. The fundamental principles of the Code are set out in Part 1. They include the principle that, wherever possible and subject to the views of parents, children with special educational needs should be educated in mainstream schools. They also include the principle of partnership. If effective provision is to be made for children with special educational needs, it is essential that schools, LEAs, the health services, social services, voluntary organisations and other agencies work very closely with each other, and that all work closely with parents.

17. The Department for Education and the Welsh Office are issuing and distributing widely a Guide for Parents on special educational needs. That Guide, like the Code, lays particular emphasis on partnership. The knowledge, views and experiences of parents are vital if effective provision is to be made for their children.

The SEN Tribunal

18. The Code's guidance is designed to promote partnership. Nonetheless, it is important that, where agreement cannot be reached, parents should have access to a quick and independent system of appeal against LEAs' decisions about assessments and statements. The 1993 Act therefore establishes a new SEN Tribunal and extends parents' rights of appeal as originally set out in the 1981 Act. The Code describes all these rights of appeal, while the Guide for Parents gives basic information about how parents should approach the Tribunal. The Tribunal will be publishing information to parents about its operation. Its rules and procedures will be set out in regulations.

19. When considering an appeal, the Tribunal must have regard to any provision of the Code of Practice which is relevant to any question arising on the appeal. The existence of the Tribunal and parents' new extended rights of appeal will serve as an added incentive to LEAs to have regard to the Code. However, the Tribunal will not exercise a general oversight of LEAs' adherence to the Code's provisions. The Tribunal's task is to consider whether LEAs have reached the right decision in the particular circumstances. Nonetheless, the Tribunal will expect LEAs to be able to justify any departure from the Code where such a departure was relevant to the decision in question.

Relevant Regulations and Circulars

20. The following Regulations are also relevant to matters covered in the Code:

i. the Education (Special Educational Needs) Regulations 1994, which are attached to the Code

ii. the Education (Special Educational Needs) (Information) Regulations 1994, which are summarised in the Code and attached to and enlarged upon in the Circular on the Organisation of Special Educational Provision, which is published alongside the Code, and

iii. the Education (Payment for Special Educational Needs Supplies) Regulations 1994, which are also covered in the Circular on the Organisation of Special Educational Provision.

21. Also relevant is a package of six Circulars on 'Pupils with Problems'. This includes Circulars on:

- pupil behaviour and discipline

- the education of children with emotional and behavioural difficulties

- exclusions from school

- the education by LEAs of children otherwise than at school

- the education of sick children, and

- the education of children being looked after by local authorities.

22. The Code of Practice and the Circulars mentioned above replace:

- DES Circular 22/89 (Welsh Office Circular 54/89) and its addendum on Assessments and Statements of Special Educational Needs: Procedures within the Education, Health and Social Services

- DES Circular 23/89 (Welsh Office Circular 61/89) on Special Schools for Pupils with Emotional and Behavioural Difficulties

- Ministry of Education Circular No.312 on The Education of Patients in Hospital, and

- DES Circular letter 1/73 (Welsh Office Circular 194/73 and DH Circular 42/73) on Education in Community Homes.

Code of Practice on the Identification and Assessment of Special Educational Needs

Contents

3. STATUTORY ASSESSMENT OF SPECIAL EDUCATIONAL NEEDS

Code of Practice on the Identification and Assessment of Special Educational Needs

1. Introduction: Principles and Procedures

1:1. To enable pupils with special educational needs to benefit as fully as possible from their education presents teachers, and all the professionals and administrators involved, with some of the most challenging and rewarding work the education service can offer. Much has been achieved by schools and local education authorities (LEAs) in enabling children with special educational needs to lead full and productive lives. The purpose of this Code of Practice, which benefits from this experience, is to give practical guidance to LEAs and the governing bodies of all maintained schools – and to all those who help them, including the health services and social services – on the discharge of their functions under Part III of the Education Act l993.

1:2. The fundamental principles of the Code are that:

- **the needs of all pupils who may have special educational needs either throughout, or at any time during, their school careers must be addressed; the Code recognises that there is a continuum of needs and a continuum of provision, which may be made in a wide variety of different forms**

- **children with special educational needs require the greatest possible access to a broad and balanced education, including the National Curriculum**

- **the needs of most pupils will be met in the mainstream, and without a statutory assessment or statement of special educational needs. Children with special educational needs, including children with statements of special educational needs, should, where appropriate and taking into account the wishes of their parents, be educated alongside their peers in mainstream schools**

- **even before he or she reaches compulsory school age a child may have special educational needs requiring the intervention of the LEA as well as the health services**

- **the knowledge, views and experience of parents are vital. Effective assessment and provision will be secured where there is the greatest possible degree of partnership between parents and their children and schools, LEAs and other agencies.**

1:3. The practices and procedures essential in pursuit of these principles are that:

- **all children with special educational needs should be identified and assessed as early as possible and as quickly as is consistent with thoroughness**

- provision for all children with special educational needs should be made by the most appropriate agency. In most cases this will be the child's mainstream school, working in partnership with the child's parents: no statutory assessment will be necessary

- where needed, LEAs must make assessments and statements in accordance with the prescribed time limits; must write clear and thorough statements, setting out the child's educational and non-educational needs, the objectives to be secured, the provision to be made and the arrangements for monitoring and review; and ensure the annual review of the special educational provision arranged for the child and the updating and monitoring of educational targets

- special educational provision will be most effective when those responsible take into account the ascertainable wishes of the child concerned, considered in the light of his or her age and understanding

- there must be close cooperation between all the agencies concerned and a multi-disciplinary approach to the resolution of issues.

1:4. The detailed guidance which follows in the rest of the Code is subject to these principles, practices and procedures, and must be read with them kept clearly in mind. The Code recommends the general adoption of a staged model of special educational needs. The first three stages are based in the school, which will, as necessary, call upon the help of external specialists. At stages 4 and 5 the LEA share responsibility with schools:

Stage 1: class or subject teachers identify or register a child's special educational needs and, consulting the school's SEN coordinator (see Glossary), take initial action

Stage 2: the school's SEN coordinator takes lead responsibility for gathering information and for coordinating the child's special educational provision, working with the child's teachers

Stage 3: teachers and the SEN coordinator are supported by specialists from outside the school

Stage 4: the LEA consider the need for a statutory assessment and, if appropriate, make a multidisciplinary assessment

Stage 5: the LEA consider the need for a statement of special educational needs and, if appropriate, make a statement and arrange, monitor and review provision.

1:5. There is scope for differences of definition of the stages in such a model and for variation in the number of stages adopted by schools and LEAs. The Code does not prescribe definitions and does not insist that there must always be five stages. But the Code does advise that the adoption of a model which recognises the various levels of need, the different responsibilities to assess and meet those needs, and the associated variations in provision, will best reflect and promote common recognition of the continuum of special educational needs. Schools and LEAs will need to be able to demonstrate, in their arrangements for children with special educational needs, that they are fulfilling their statutory duty to have regard to this Code. In the case of schools, OFSTED and OHMCI (Wales) inspection teams will consider the effectiveness of schools' policies and practices and the extent to which schools have had regard to the Code.

1:6. The ordering of the guidance reflects the consideration that it should be read as a whole, so that a full picture can be gained of the various parts of the processes, the roles of all concerned, and the particular considerations affecting the treatment of children at different stages in their lives and school careers. The format of the document is:

Part 1: Introduction: Principles and procedures

Part 2: Stages 1-3: School-based stages of assessment and provision

Part 3: Stage 4: Statutory assessments

Part 4: Stage 5: Statements

Part 5: Children under five with special educational needs

Part 6: The annual review of statements.

1:7. The Code thus starts with the school-based stages of assessment and provision since some general issues can most appropriately be addressed in this Part. That should not, however, be taken to diminish the importance of addressing needs as early as possible, such as at the pre-school stage when appropriate, as explained in Part 5. Nor should the emphasis on the work of mainstream schools be seen to diminish the importance of the work of or the relevance of the Code to special schools (see Glossary). Throughout, the law on which the Code offers guidance is summarised in lined boxes with the text in light blue: except where stated otherwise, references to 'the Act' are to the Education Act 1993; references to 'sections' are references to sections in the Act; references to 'the Regulations' are to the Education (Special Educational Needs) Regulations 1994.

1:8. Bodies helping children with special educational needs and their parents in Wales should bear in mind that the Welsh Language Act 1993 (see Glossary) has the fundamental principle that the Welsh language should be treated on the basis of equality with the English language. All bodies serving the public in Wales are required to agree schemes setting out the services they provide, and intend to provide, through the medium of Welsh. In their dealings particularly with parents, those bodies should remember the requirements of the Welsh Language Act and the need to communicate in the language preferred by parents.

2. School-based Stages of Assessment and Provision

Introduction

2:1. At the heart of the work of every school and every class lies a cycle of planning, teaching and assessing. These general arrangements in a school take account of the wide range of abilities, aptitudes and interests that children bring to school. The majority of children will learn and progress within these arrangements. Those who have difficulty in so doing may have special educational needs:

A child has *special educational needs* if he or she has a *learning difficulty* which calls for *special educational provision* to be made for him or her.

A child has a *learning difficulty* if he or she:

(a) has a significantly greater difficulty in learning than the majority of children of the same age

(b) has a disability which either prevents or hinders the child from making use of educational facilities of a kind provided for children of the same age in schools within the area of the local education authority

(c) is under five and falls within the definition at (a) or (b) above or would do if special educational provision was not made for the child.

A child must not be regarded as having a learning difficulty solely because the language or form of language of the home is different from the language in which he or she is or will be taught.

Special educational provision means:

(a) for a child over two, educational provision which is additional to, or otherwise different from, the educational provision made generally for children of the child's age in maintained schools, other than special schools, in the area

(b) for a child under two, educational provision of any kind.

(Section 156)

2:2. Nationally, about 20 per cent of children may have some form of special educational needs at some time. For the vast majority of children such needs will be met by their school – with outside help if necessary – and school governing bodies have statutory responsibilities to ensure that those needs are met. Only in a small minority of cases – nationally, around two per cent of children – will a child have special educational needs of a severity or complexity which requires the LEA to determine and arrange the special educational provision for the child by means of a statutory statement of special educational needs. These figures are broad national estimates: the proportion of children with special educational needs varies significantly from area to area.

2:3. This Part contains guidance designed to help schools fulfil their statutory duties towards pupils with special educational needs. These statutory duties are set out at paragraph 2:6 below. They are cast in broad terms. The precise way in which they are fulfilled is a matter for schools themselves to decide in the light of the Code, which is designed to help schools make effective decisions.

2:4. The guidance in this Part applies to schools in general – primary and secondary, LEA-maintained and grant-maintained. The broad principles apply also to nursery schools and classes. Schools should, of course, consider the Code in the light of their particular circumstances, for example their phase, organisation, size, location and pupil population, and in the light of their policy for the allocation of resources to pupils with special educational needs. It is not expected that all schools, having considered the Code, will adopt identical approaches. But all schools must have regard to what this Code says.

2:5. This Part deals first with the general arrangements which schools should make, and second with the procedures which might be followed for an individual child.

The duties of governing bodies

2:6. School governing bodies have important statutory duties towards pupils with special educational needs:

The governing body must

- **do their best to secure that the necessary provision is made for any pupil who has special educational needs**

- **secure that, where the 'responsible person' – the head teacher or the appropriate governor – has been informed by the LEA that a pupil has special educational needs, those needs are made known to all who are likely to teach him or her**

- **secure that teachers in the school are aware of the importance of identifying, and providing for, those pupils who have special educational needs**

- **consult the LEA; as appropriate, the Funding Authority (see Glossary); and the governing bodies of other schools, when it seems to them necessary or desirable in the interests of coordinated special educational provision in the area as a whole**

- **report annually to parents on the school's policy for pupils with special educational needs**

- **ensure that the pupil joins in the activities of the school together with pupils who do not have special educational needs, so far as that is reasonably practical and compatible with the pupil receiving the necessary special educational provision, the efficient education of other children in the school and the efficient use of resources**

(Section 161)

- **have regard to this Code of Practice when carrying out their duties toward all pupils with special educational needs.**

(Section 157)

Roles and responsibilities in mainstream schools

2:7. Provision for pupils with special educational needs is a matter for the school as a whole. In addition to the governing body, the school's head teacher, SEN coordinator or team, and all other members of staff have important responsibilities. In practice the division of responsibility is a matter for individual schools, to be decided in the light of a school's circumstances and size, priorities and ethos. But schools should bear in mind the following:

- **the governing body** should, in cooperation with the head teacher, determine the school's general policy and approach to provision for children with special educational needs, establish the appropriate staffing and funding arrangements and maintain a general oversight of the school's work

- **the governing body** may appoint a **committee** to take a particular interest in and closely monitor the school's work on behalf of children with special educational needs

- **the head teacher** has responsibility for the day-to-day **management** of all aspects of the school's work, including provision for children with special educational needs. He or she will keep the governing body fully informed. At the same time, the head teacher will work closely with the school's SEN coordinator or team

- **the SEN coordinator or team**, working closely with their fellow teachers, has responsibility for the day-to-day **operation** of the school's SEN policy and for coordinating provision for pupils with special educational needs, particularly at stages 2 and 3

- **all teaching and non-teaching staff** should be involved in the development of the school's SEN policy and be fully aware of the school's procedures for identifying, assessing and making provision for pupils with special educational needs.

2:8. Whatever arrangements are made in a particular school, statutory duties remain with the governing body.

The 'responsible person' means the head teacher or the appropriate governor: that is the chairman of the governing body unless the governing body have designated another governor for the purpose. In the case of a nursery school, the responsible person is the head teacher.

(Section 161 (2))

2:9. The chairman of the governing body, a member of that body's SEN committee or the head teacher will have the role of 'responsible person' (see Glossary). The LEA should inform that person when they conclude that a pupil at the school has special educational needs, for example following the making of a statement or when a child with a statement moves from another school. The responsible person must then ensure that all those who will teach the child know about his or her special educational needs. The responsible person should also endorse any request made by the school to the LEA for a statutory assessment – see paragraph 2:115 below.

The school's SEN policy

2:10. As part of their statutory duties, governing bodies of all maintained schools (see Glossary) must publish information about, and report on, the school's policy on special educational needs. While the governing body and the head teacher will take overall responsibility for the school's SEN policy, the school as a whole should be involved in its development. The school may also wish to consult the LEA, the Funding Authority as appropriate, and neighbouring schools when they first draw up the policy and when they later consider any significant revisions to it, in the interests of coordinated special educational provision within the area as a whole. The Education (Special Educational Needs) (Information) Regulations 1994 prescribe the information which schools must make available. Mainstream schools must provide:

1. **Basic information about the school's special educational provision:**
   - the objectives of the school's SEN policy
   - the name of the school's SEN coordinator or teacher responsible for the day-to-day operation of the SEN policy
   - the arrangements for coordinating educational provision for pupils with SEN
   - admission arrangements
   - any SEN specialism and any special units
   - any special facilities which increase or assist access to the school by pupils with SEN

2. **Information about the school's policies for identification, assessment and provision for all pupils with SEN:**
   - the allocation of resources to and amongst pupils with SEN
   - identification and assessment arrangements; and review procedures
   - arrangements for providing access for pupils with SEN to a balanced and broadly based curriculum, including the National Curriculum
   - how children with special educational needs are integrated within the school as a whole
   - criteria for evaluating the success of the school's SEN policy
   - arrangements for considering complaints about special educational provision within the school

3. **Information about the school's staffing policies and partnership with bodies beyond the schools:**
   - the school's arrangements for SEN in-service training
   - use made of teachers and facilities from outside the school, including support services
   - arrangements for partnership with parents
   - links with other mainstream schools and special schools, including arrangements when pupils change schools or leave school
   - links with health and social services, educational welfare services and any voluntary organisations.

Education (Special Educational Needs) (Information) Regulations, regulation 2 and Schedule 1

> The annual report for each school shall include a report containing such information as may be prescribed about the implementation of the governing body's policy for pupils with special educational needs.
>
> (Section 161(5))

2:11. The governing body's report must include information on:

> - the success of the SEN policy
> - significant changes in the policy
> - any consultation with the LEA, the Funding Authority and other schools
> - how resources have been allocated to and amongst children with special educational needs over the year.
>
> Education (Special Educational Needs) (Information) Regulations, regulation 5 and Schedule 4

2:12. In commenting on the success of the policy, the report should demonstrate the effectiveness of the school's systems for:

- identification
- assessment
- provision
- monitoring and record-keeping
- use of outside support services and agencies

2:13. In considering the effectiveness of the school's work on behalf of children with special educational needs and in drawing up their annual report, the governing body may wish to consult other schools and the support services used by the school. The school should consider whether amendments to their policy are needed in the light of this evaluation.

The SEN coordinator

2:14. In all mainstream schools a designated teacher should be responsible for:

- the day-to-day operation of the school's SEN policy
- liaising with and advising fellow teachers
- coordinating provision for children with special educational needs

- **maintaining the school's SEN register and overseeing the records on all pupils with special educational needs (see paragraph 2:25)**

- **liaising with parents of children with special educational needs**

- **contributing to the in-service training of staff**

- **liaising with external agencies including the educational psychology service and other support agencies, medical and social services and voluntary bodies.**

2:15. This is the role of the SEN coordinator. In a small school, one person may take on this role, possibly the head or deputy. In larger schools, there may be an SEN coordinating or learning support team. The time and attention which the SEN coordinator is able to devote to his or her responsibilities will depend upon the circumstances of particular schools. Governing bodies and head teachers may need to give careful thought to the SEN coordinator's timetable in the light of this Code and in the context of resources available to the school.

Identification and assessment

2:16. The importance of early identification, assessment and provision for any child who may have special educational needs cannot be over-emphasised. The earlier action is taken, the more responsive the child is likely to be, and the more readily can intervention be made without undue disruption to the organisation of the school, including the delivery of the curriculum for that particular child. If a difficulty proves transient the child will subsequently be able to learn and progress normally. If the child's difficulties prove less responsive to provision made by the school, then an early start can be made in considering the additional provision that may be needed to support the child's progress.

2:17. To assist in the early identification of children with special educational needs, the school will wish to make use of any appropriate screening or assessment tools which, along with the assessment of children within the National Curriculum, enable the school to consider children's achievements and progress. Schools should make full use of information passed to them when the pupil transfers between phases. Schools should also be open and responsive to expressions of concern and information provided by parents.

2:18. The identification and assessment of the special educational needs of children from minority ethnic groups, including children whose first language is not English or Welsh, requires very careful consideration. Lack of competence in English or Welsh must not be equated with learning difficulties as understood in this Code. Care should be taken to consider the child within the context of his or her home, language, culture and community; to ensure, if necessary by the use of bilingual support staff, interpreters and translators, that the child and his or her parents fully understand the measures the school is taking; and, so far as possible, to use assessment tools which are culturally neutral and useful for a range of ethnic groups. Schools should make use of any local sources of advice relevant to the ethnic group concerned.

2:19. Effective management, disciplinary and pastoral arrangements and policies in schools can help prevent some special educational needs arising, and minimise others. Differentation of class work within a common curriculum framework will help the school to meet the learning needs of all children. Schools should not automatically assume that children's learning difficulties always result solely or even mainly from problems within the child. The school's practices can make a difference – for good or ill. The governing body, head teacher and SEN coordinator should be alert to any particular patterns in the school's identification and registration of children's special educational needs or parents' expressions of concern and should examine the school's general practices and policies in the light of any such patterns.

The five-stage model

2:20. To give specific help to children who have special educational needs, schools should adopt a staged response. This approach recognises that there is a continuum of special educational needs and, where necessary, brings increasing specialist expertise to bear on the difficulties that a child may be experiencing.

2:21 This Code sets out a **five-stage model** – see paragraph 1:4. Responsibility for pupils within stages 1-3 lies with the school, although the LEA will be closely involved at stage 3. The LEA and the school share responsibility at stages 4 and 5.

2:22. Some schools and LEAs may adopt different models, for example a four-stage approach, with the school taking responsibility for stages 1 and 2, the LEA and the school sharing responsibility at stages 3 and 4. It is not essential that there should be five stages. It is important, however, that there should be differentiation between the stages, which should aim to match the action taken on behalf of a child to his or her needs.

2:23. The majority of children will not pass through all three school-based stages of assessment and provision. In many cases action taken at one stage will mean that the child will not have to move on to the next. Only for those children whose progress continues to cause concern at any one stage will the school need to move to the next stage. A relatively large proportion of children may be helped by the stage 1 procedures. Smaller proportions may be at stages 2 or 3. A very small number of children may fail to progress even with support at stage 3. For such children the school should consider referral to the LEA with a view to a statutory assessment: information on the child's learning difficulty and the special educational provision made by the school, assisted by external agencies, up to and including stage 3, will form an important part of the evidence to be considered by the LEA in deciding whether to make a statutory assessment at stage 4.

2:24. These stages will not usually be steps on the way to statutory assessment. Nor are they hurdles to be crossed before a statutory assessment can be made. They are means of helping schools and parents decide what special educational provision is necessary and to match that provision to the child's needs. It is for the school, consulting parents, to decide what stage is suitable for a child. If a child's needs require action at stage 2 or 3, even if no action has previously been taken at stage 1, then action should be taken at stage 2 or 3.

Record keeping

2:25. Schools should keep a **register** of all children with special educational needs. They should also record the steps taken to meet the needs of individual children. The school's SEN coordinator should have responsibility for ensuring that the register and records are properly kept and available as needed. Records at each stage will inform the school's approach at the next. If schools refer a child for a statutory assessment, they should make available to the LEA a record of their work with the child. LEAs and schools should consider the use of agreed pro-formas for recording work with children with special educational needs at stages 1, 2 and 3: this can be particularly helpful in ensuring that information is effectively transferred between schools.

The in-service training of staff

2:26. The school's SEN policy should describe plans for the in-service training and professional development of staff to help them work effectively with pupils with special educational needs. The SEN in-service training policy should be part of the school's development plan and should, where appropriate, cover the needs of non-teaching assistants and other staff. Schools should consider the training needs of the SEN coordinator and how he or she can be equipped to provide training for fellow teachers. Schools and LEAs should also consider governing bodies' in-service training needs in the light of this Code. A school contemplating a particular special educational needs in-service training programme may wish to inform itself of the LEA's in-service training policy and may also wish to consult other schools in the area with a view to securing economies of scale and sharing expertise.

Working with others

2:27. The effective implementation of the school-based stages of assessment and provision will be possible only if schools create positive working relationships with parents, pupils, the health services and the local authority social services department (SSD), as well as with LEAs and any other providers of support services. Many children with special educational needs have a range of difficulties and the achievement of educational objectives is likely to be delayed without partnership between all concerned.

Partnership with parents

2:28. The relationship between parents of children with special educational needs and the school which their child is attending has a crucial bearing on the child's educational progress and the effectiveness of any school-based action. Most schools already have effective working relationships with parents, including the parents of children with special educational needs. School-based arrangements should ensure that assessment reflects a sound and comprehensive knowledge of a child and his or her responses to a variety of carefully planned and recorded actions which take account of the wishes, feelings and knowledge of parents at all stages. Children's progress will be diminished if their parents are not seen as partners in the educational process with unique knowledge and information to impart. Professional help can seldom be wholly effective unless it builds upon parents' capacity to be involved and unless parents consider that professionals take account of what they say and treat their views and anxieties as intrinsically important.

2:29. The school-based stages should therefore utilise parents' own distinctive knowledge and skills and contribute to parents' own understanding of how best to help their child. The identification of a special educational need may be alarming to parents. In some instances parents may consider that their early concerns were given insufficient attention. Schools should not interpret a failure to participate as indicating a lack of interest or willingness. Parents may feel they are being blamed for their child's difficulties when the school first raises questions with them. Nonetheless, schools should make every effort to encourage parents to recognise that they have responsibilities towards their child, and that the most effective provision will be made when they are open and confident in working in partnership with the school and with professionals.

2:30. If the child has a behavioural difficulty or is following a developmental activity of any kind which requires a structured approach in school, reinforcement at home by parents will be crucial. Many parents can become discouraged by their child's continuing difficulties at home and at school, and feel themselves to be inadequate in dealing with the difficulty. The governing body, head teacher and the SEN coordinator should consider how the school can support such parents.

2:31. Some parents may have problems in understanding written information and communicating with schools because of literacy difficulties or if English or Welsh is not their first language. The school should consider how best to involve such parents, and whether to make written information available in the main languages of the local community, using the resources of relevant community-based organisations. In some instances taped or videotaped information packs may be helpful, particularly in illustrating the type of provision and support which is available, and how parents may help their children at home.

2:32. Schools should be aware of the definitions of 'parent' and 'parental responsibility', which are in the Glossary. They should know in each instance who should be regarded as a parent of a particular child and who should therefore be consulted regarding the child's progress in school. It is often the case that adults in more than one household qualify as parents for the purposes of the Education Acts. All those with parental responsibility for a child have rights and responsibilities towards the child: a school should endeavour to keep records of all those with parental responsibility and involve them as much as possible in the child's education. However, this will not always be practical and a school may be able to discharge its responsibilities by dealing with the parent who has day-to-day care of the child. Where parents disagree among themselves about decisions regarding their child's education, they can apply to the Court for resolution under the Children Act 1989.

2:33. A school's arrangements for parents of children with special educational needs should include:

Information

- ■ on the school's SEN policy
- ■ on the support available for children with special educational needs within the school and LEA
- ■ on parents' involvement in assessment and decision-making, emphasising the importance of their contribution
- ■ on services such as those provided by the local authority for children 'in need'
- ■ on local and national voluntary organisations which might provide information, advice or counselling

Partnership

- ■ arrangements for recording and acting upon parental concerns
- ■ procedures for involving parents when a concern is first expressed within the school
- ■ arrangements for incorporating parents' views in assessment and subsequent reviews

Access for parents

- ■ information in a range of community languages
- ■ information on tape for parents who may have literacy or communication difficulties
- ■ a parents' room or other arrangements in the school to help parents feel confident and comfortable.

Involving the child

2:34. The effectiveness of any assessment and intervention will be influenced by the involvement and interest of the child or young person concerned.

2:35. The benefits are:

- ■ practical – children have important and relevant information. Their support is crucial to the effective implementation of any individual education programme
- ■ principle – children have a right to be heard. They should be encouraged to participate in decision-making about provision to meet their special educational needs.

2:36. Schools should, therefore, make every effort to identify the ascertainable views and wishes of the child or young person about his or her current and future education. Positive pupil involvement is unlikely to happen spontaneously. Careful attention, guidance and encouragement will be required to help pupils respond relevantly and fully. Young people are more likely to respond positively to intervention programmes if they fully understand the rationale for their involvement and if they are given some personal responsibility for their own progress. Schools should, for example, discuss the purpose of a particular assessment arrangement with the child; invite comments from the child; and consider the use of pupil reports and systematic feedback to the child concerned. Many children with special educational needs have little self-confidence and low self-esteem. Involving children in tracking their own progress within a programme designed to meet their particular learning or behavioural difficulty can contribute to an improved self-image and greater self-confidence.

2:37. Schools should consider how they:

- **involve pupils in decision-making processes**

- **determine the pupil's level of participation, taking into account approaches to assessment and intervention which are suitable for his or her age, ability and past experiences**

- **record pupils' views in identifying their difficulties, setting goals, agreeing a development strategy, monitoring and reviewing progress**

- **involve pupils in implementing individual education plans.**

Cooperation between LEAs, the health services and social services

2:38. Effective action on behalf of children with special educational needs will often depend upon close cooperation between schools, LEAs, the health services and the social services departments of local authorities. The Children Act 1989 and the Education Act 1993 place duties on these bodies to help each other:

District health authorities, LEAs, grant maintained schools and City Technology Colleges must comply with a request from a social services department for assistance in providing services for *children in need*, so long as the request is compatible with their duties and does not unduly prejudice the discharge of any of their functions.

(Children Act 1989, section 27)

Social services departments, subject to a qualification similar to that in section 27 above, and district health authorities, subject to the reasonableness of the request in the light of available resources, must comply with a request for help from an LEA in connection with *children with special educational needs*, unless they consider that the help is not necessary for the exercise of the LEA's functions.

(Education Act 1993, section 166)

2:39. Information which a maintained school must make available must include the school's arrangements for working in partnership with the health services, social services, the education welfare service and any relevant local and national voluntary organisations. As explained below, schools' first point of contact with the health services will usually be the school doctor or the child's general practitioner. This doctor will usually be able to advise the school but, if a problem is confirmed, should also tell the medical officer designated to work with children with special educational needs that the school has sought advice about a child. Schools' first point of contact with social services will usually be with an officer similarly designated to work with schools and LEAs on behalf of children with special educational needs.

2:40. In order to achieve full collaboration at both school and local authority level, representatives of LEAs, social services departments and the health services may choose to meet on a reasonably regular basis to plan and coordinate activity. Such arrangements will vary according to local circumstances, but the principles of partnership and close working relationships between agencies, supported by meetings to discuss both strategic and operational issues, will have general application.

Child health services

2:41. A child's difficulty at school may be related to a medical condition, disability or developmental delay, which might be first identified by the child's general practitioner, health visitor, therapist, the school health service, community paediatrician or through a teacher's or parent's expression of anxiety about an aspect of the child's health and development.

2:42. When schools first suspect a medical problem they should, having obtained the consent of the child's parents, consult the school doctor or the child's general practitioner. If a problem is confirmed, the doctor consulted should in turn notify the medical officer designated by the district health authority (DHA) to work with the LEA on behalf of children with special educational needs and to lead the DHA's contribution to the statutory assessment process. If the designated officer is given early information about a child, he or she will be able to respond quickly and within the statutory time limits to any later request from the LEA for advice in the making of a statutory assessment.

2:43. How the health services contribute to the identification of children with special educational needs will depend upon the role of the family's general practitioner and the contractual arrangements which the DHA have with providers of health services for children. Almost all of these providers will be one of the following types of NHS Trusts:

- acute hospital Trusts responsible for hospital services for children

- community Trusts with responsibility for children's services provided outside hospital

- combined acute and community Trusts who, in addition to hospital services, also manage child development centres and child health clinics.

Any of these Trusts may employ the staff – consultant paediatricians, consultant community paediatricians, clinical medical officers (many of whom are school doctors) from whom the DHA will need to designate a medical officer for special educational needs.

2:44. The role of the general practitioner will largely depend on whether he or she has provided the medical input to the programme of pre-school child health surveillance which is delivered at child health clinics and, increasingly, within GP practices. A GP who has accepted a child for child health surveillance will be best equipped to provide an initial medical report for children up to age five. Elsewhere clinical medical officers, who usually work in clinics and in the school health service, and health visitors and school nurses may be capable of providing fuller information.

2:45. With the introduction of the contractual arrangements for the purchase and provision of health services referred to at paragraph 2:43, the designated medical officer for special educational needs will have a strategic and operational role in coordinating activity across DHAs, NHS Trusts and GP fund holders.

2:46. At the strategic level, the designated medical officer should check that the DHA have arrangements for ensuring that the Trusts and GPs providing child health services:

■ **inform LEAs of children who they think may have special educational needs (paragraph 5:13)**

■ **provide medical advice to LEAs for the assessment of children within the prescribed time limits (paragraphs 3:33 and 3.34)**

■ **consider, with LEAs and with regard to available resources, the health services' contribution to the non-educational provision to be specified in a statement (paragraph 4:32).**

2:47. At the operational level, the designated medical officer should:

■ **ensure that all schools have a contact (usually the school doctor) for seeking medical advice on children who may have special educational needs**

■ **provide a resource to other health service staff – for example, GPs and therapists – who require assistance in preparing reports on the medical history and health needs of children for schools and LEAs**

■ **coordinate the health services' advice for a statutory assessment and, frequently, participate in multi-agency meetings on assessments and making statements**

■ **coordinate the provision to be made by the health services for a child with special educational needs when, as may be the case with therapy and nursing services, either a DHA or GP fund holder may be responsible for the purchasing of these services.**

2:48. Conditions such as a hearing loss or a visual impairment may, if undiagnosed, lead to the child losing interest and becoming alienated. Even when a child's known medical condition, such as asthma or epilepsy, is effectively managed by medication, there may still be secondary effects, or treatment may lead to occasional side effects, which may in turn influence the child's ability to participate fully in classroom activities.

2:49. Other children may be receiving treatment for diseases, such as childhood cancers, which will periodically affect their ability to participate fully in the school's curriculum and other arrangements, and which may necessitate periods of time away from school. Children with identified medical needs will not necessarily have an associated learning difficulty, but the consequences of their illness or condition (often associated with parental anxiety) may lead to future difficulties if there is not close collaboration between the school, the relevant child health services, and parents. Parents should always be fully involved and should be asked to give their consent to consultation with relevant health professionals.

2:50. Children's progress may also be affected by emotional and behavioural difficulties. In some instances these may be related to periods of depression (which may be short-term and related to illness of the child or within the family) or other mental health problems. Schools may also identify children or young people who are showing signs of eating disorders such as anorexia or bulimia. Children may also be affected by peer relationships such as bullying or difficulties in establishing personal relationships. These may be associated with a range of emotional and social difficulties and have a potentially serious effect on the child's future health, development and education. Schools should ensure that their own pastoral care arrangements allow children and young people to discuss any health-related and other problems with a relevant health professional, educational psychologist, education welfare officer (see Glossary) or other professional, and that the school and family liaise in providing maximum support for the child.

2:51. The head teacher, consulting the SEN coordinator, should ensure the confidentiality and effectiveness of systems operated by the school for:

■ **keeping any medical information and reports on children with special educational needs**

■ **drawing together further information that may be available from, for example:**

> **general practitioners**
> **the school health service**
> **health visitors**
> **community nursing services**
> **community paediatricians**
> **child and adolescent mental health services**
> **hospital children's departments**
> **physiotherapy or speech and language therapy services**

■ **the transfer of relevant medical information between phases**

■ **ensuring, through cooperation with health professionals, the elimination of underlying medical causes as a possible explanation for observable learning and behaviour difficulties**

■ **identifying early signs of depression, abnormal eating behaviour, and substance misuse.**

2:52. No doctor or other health service worker should disclose medical information without first obtaining the consent of the parents and, where he or she has sufficient understanding, the child. Exceptionally, children under age 16, who are judged to be competent by their doctors, may give consent independently of their parents. When they first form an opinion that a child has special educational needs, doctors may find it convenient to alert parents and children to the possibility that they will be asked to give information to schools and the LEA. Doctors may then seek the consent of parents and children to the disclosure of necessary medical information to the school or LEA if they judge this would be helpful to the child.

Social services and education welfare service involvement

2:53. Schools should be aware of the full range of local services provided by the education welfare service and by social services departments. SSDs have duties under section 17 of the Children Act 1989 to provide a range of services for children regarded as being 'in need' (see Glossary). While a child with special educational needs will not necessarily be 'in need' as defined in the Children Act, that Act allows an integrated approach to the educational, health and welfare needs of children with special educational needs who are 'in need'. It also requires schools to cooperate with social services departments if a child is 'in need' (section 27 of the Children Act) or at risk of significant harm, for example, abuse (section 47 of the Children Act), although this would not automatically mean that the child had special educational needs.

2:54. Social services departments should designate an officer or officers who are responsible for working with schools and LEAs on behalf of children with special educational needs and to whom schools and LEAs should refer for advice. If the designated officer has early information about a child, the social services department will be able to react quickly, and within the statutory time limits, to any later request from the LEA for advice in the making of a statutory assessment. Social services departments should ensure that all schools in the area know the name of, and how to contact, a designated social services officer who has responsibilities for special educational needs.

2:55. If a child is being looked after by the local authority – that is where the child is in residential care or a foster family placement or using a respite care facility – the local authority social services department will maintain a child care plan which will include information on the educational arrangements made for the child including any special needs he or she may have, and which will involve parents and the child in forward planning. Children living away from home may have had disrupted school lives because of frequent moves. They may also have experienced trauma as a result of family breakdown or ill-health and the disruption of moving from a known area and trusted professionals, for example in a local school.

2:56. Such children, and those who have experienced homelessness with frequent moves between short-term accommodation, will need careful observation and support. Schools should make every effort to ensure that any difficulties are promptly identified and if possible dealt with in the school, and should acknowledge the emotional consequences for some children of living away from family or friends. Both the education welfare service and social services departments should be able to contribute to realistic planning and parental involvement in the resolution of any difficulties. Schools should consider whether the child's teacher or the school's SEN coordinator should attend the child's care plan review. In some instances children may have missed developmental or health checks, and the school health service should be consulted if there is any doubt about the child's health or well-being, and to ensure that there is no remediable sensory or other impairment or medical condition which is contributing to any difficulties the child has in school. For further information, see the Circular: 'The Education of Children Being Looked After By Local Authorities'.

2:57. Schools should therefore have suitable arrangements for:

- **liaising with social services**
- **registering a concern about a child's welfare**
- **putting into practice any local procedures relating to child protection issues**
- **liaising with the local authority when a child is looked after by that authority**
- **obtaining information on services provided by the local authority for children 'in need'.**

Special educational needs support services

2:58. Special educational needs support services can play an important part in helping schools identify, assess and make provision for children with special educational needs. Such services include specialist teachers of children with hearing, visual, and speech and language impairments, teachers in more general learning and behaviour support services, educational psychologists and advisers or teachers with a knowledge of information technology for children with special educational needs.

2:59. Schools should work in close partnership with the providers of such services. The SEN coordinator, in particular, should be aware of the LEA's policy for the provision of support services and how the school can secure access to them. LEAs should provide full information to all schools in their area about the range of services locally available and how they can be secured. Whether or not funding for particular support services is delegated to schools, it may be helpful for schools and LEAs to make service level agreements for such services, specifying the scope, quality and duration of the service. When schools enter into contracts with private or voluntary sector providers, they should satisfy themselves of the qualifications and experience of the specialists involved and that the service represents good value for money.

2:60. Schools should always consult specialists when they take action on behalf of a child at stage 3. But the involvement of specialists need not be confined to stage 3. Outside specialists can play an important part in the very early identification of special educational needs and in advising schools on effective provision which can prevent the development of more significant needs.

School-based Stages

2:61. The school-based stages should be seen as a continuous and systematic cycle of planning, action and review within the school to enable the child with special educational needs to learn and progress. As such, they are a natural extension of the work of schools with children generally.

2:62. Paragraphs 2:65–2:120 set out one model of a staged approach to the identification, assessment, monitoring and review of the special educational needs of children without statements in mainstream schools. These paragraphs offer guidance as to what schools might do, particularly the procedures they might adopt, in order to fulfil their duty to use their best endeavours on behalf of children with special educational needs but without statements.

2:63. Good practice can take many different forms. It is for individual schools to decide the exact procedures they should adopt and, of course, for individual schools to decide the nature and content of special educational provision that they should make.

2:64. Schools should consult the LEA when considering the development of a staged approach or any significant changes to such an approach. Some schools may choose to use a two-stage model, perhaps combining elements of stages 1 and 2 described below. Even those schools which decide to follow the Code's model closely may need to make adjustments to reflect their particular circumstances. The model applies to schools generally but might be adopted differently in, for example, a small rural primary school and a large inner-city comprehensive. The model nonetheless embodies certain principles which are central to this Code and to which all schools should have regard:

- **provision for a child with special educational needs should match the nature of his or her needs**

- **there should be careful recording of a child's special educational needs, the action taken and the outcomes**

- **consideration should be given to the ascertainable wishes and feelings of the child**

- **there should be close consultation and partnership with the child's parents**

- **outside specialists should be involved, particularly, but not necessarily only, in the stage preceding any referral to the LEA for a statutory assessment.**

2:65. In summary, the staged model adopted by this Code is:

Stage 1 is characterised by the gathering of information and increased differentiation within the child's normal classroom work. At this stage, the child's class teacher or form/year tutor:

- **identifies a child's special educational needs**
- **consults the child's parents and the child**

- **informs the SEN coordinator, who registers the child's special educational needs**
- **collects relevant information about the child, consulting the SEN coordinator**
- **works closely with the child in the normal classroom context**
- **monitors and reviews the child's progress.**

2:66. Stage 2 is characterised by the production of an individual education plan. At this stage, the SEN coordinator is responsible for coordinating the child's special educational provision and, always working closely with the child's teachers

- **marshals relevant information, including, as appropriate, information from sources beyond the school**
- **ensures that an individual education plan is drawn up**
- **ensures that the child's parents are informed**
- **monitors and reviews the child's progress**
- **informs the head teacher.**

2:67. Stage 3 is characterised by the involvement of specialists from outside the school. At this stage, the SEN coordinator continues to take a leading role, again working closely with the child's teachers and

- **keeps the head teacher informed**
- **draws on the advice of outside specialists, for example educational psychologists and advisory teachers**
- **ensures that the child and his or her parents are consulted**
- **ensures that an individual education plan is drawn up**
- **with outside specialists, monitors and reviews the child's progress.**

2:68. Should the child not progress satisfactorily at stage 3, outside specialists will help the school consider whether the child is likely to meet the criteria for statutory assessment by the LEA.

2:69. All schools recognise the importance of consulting parents, whether or not their children have special educational needs. They do so through a variety of means, for example parents' evenings. Those and similar occasions, for example informal discussions when the child is brought to or collected from school, can allow a school to consider a child's special educational needs with his or her parents. Formal meetings may sometimes be desirable but are not always necessary or feasible. But parents will have important information to give to the school and, working in partnership with the school, can often help their child at home. They should always be told about any special help their child receives and about the outcome of that help.

Stage 1

2:70. **Stage 1** involves the initial identification and registration of a child's special educational needs, the gathering of basic information about the child, taking early action to meet the child's needs within his or her normal classroom work and monitoring and reviewing his or her progress.

Trigger

2:71. The trigger for stage 1 is the **expression of a concern** that a child is showing signs of having special educational needs, together with the evidence for that concern, by any teacher at the school, by a parent, or by another professional, such as a health or social services worker. Such a concern would normally be expressed either to or by the child's class teacher in a primary school, or form or year tutor in a secondary school.

Roles and responsibilities

2:72. The child's class teacher or form/year tutor has overall responsibility. He or she should inform or seek advice from the SEN coordinator and consult the child's parents. The teacher may also inform the head teacher.

2:73. The child's teacher or tutor will:

- **gather information about the child and make an initial assessment of the child's special educational needs**
- **provide special help within the normal curriculum framework, exploring ways in which increased differentiation of classroom work might better meet the needs of the individual child**
- **monitor and review the child's progress.**

2:74. The SEN coordinator will:

- **ensure that the child is included in the school's SEN register**
- **help the child's teacher or tutor gather information and assess the child's needs**
- **advise and support as necessary those who will teach the child.**

Information required

2:75. The information that the child's teacher or tutor, with the help of the SEN coordinator, should collect and record at stage 1 includes:

from the school

- class records, including any from other schools which the child has attended in the previous year
- National Curriculum attainments
- standardised test results or profiles
- Records of Achievement
- reports on the child in school settings
- observations about the child's behaviour

from the parent

- views on the child's health and development
- perceptions of the child's performance, progress and behaviour at school and at home
- factors contributing to any difficulty
- action the school might take

from the child

- personal perception of any difficulties
- how they might be addressed

from other sources

- any information already available to the school from health or social services or any other source.

Assessing and meeting the child's special educational needs

2:76. The child's teacher or tutor considers how the child's special educational needs may best be addressed. The information collected at this stage will reveal:

- different perceptions of those concerned with the child
- immediate educational concerns
- the wider context of the child's learning difficulties.

2:77. On the basis of the information now available, the teacher or tutor, consulting the SEN coordinator, will decide whether:

- to continue the child's current educational arrangements, no special help being needed

  or

- to seek advice and support

  or

- to give the child special help by differentiating the curriculum and monitoring and reviewing the child's progress.

Continuing current arrangements

2:78. The expression of concern, the gathering of information, and the registration and consideration of the child's special educational needs may combine to resolve problems. It may be that no further action is needed at this stage. The teacher or tutor should record such a decision and inform the child's parents and the SEN coordinator. Even though the teacher or tutor has decided that no special educational provision is needed, the SEN coordinator should retain the child's name on the school's SEN register and consult the child's teacher or tutor about the child's progress, perhaps every term or six months, until it is clear that the child's progress is no longer likely to give any cause for concern.

Seeking advice and support

2:79. It may be clear to the child's teacher or tutor and the SEN coordinator at the outset that information additional to that available to the school is required or that action at stage 1 would be inadequate. If so, the child should move straight to the appropriate stage.

Giving special help at stage 1

2:80. The teacher or tutor, consulting the SEN coordinator, may decide that the child could benefit from a period of special attention and, in particular, carefully differentiated teaching within his or her normal classroom work. The nature and aims of such special educational provision should be recorded. The record might include:

Stage 1 – Giving special help

- **nature of concern and action to be taken**
- **targets to be achieved and monitoring arrangements**
- **review date.**

2:81. The child's parents should always be informed of the action that the school proposes to take. If it is decided to give special help at stage 1, the teacher or tutor should set a review date. This might be within a term. The teacher or tutor should tell the child's parents of this review date.

Review

2:82. The review should focus on:

- **progress made by the child**
- **effectiveness of the special help**
- **future action.**

2:83. The outcome of the review may be:

- **the child continues at stage 1:** if the child's progress has been at least satisfactory, the teacher or tutor should set targets to be achieved by the next review. If progress remains satisfactory after two reviews, the teacher or tutor may decide to increase gradually the period between reviews

- **the child no longer needs special help:** if a child's progress continues to be satisfactory within this framework of provision and review for at least two review periods, the teacher or tutor may decide that the child no longer needs special help. The SEN coordinator should retain the child's name on the SEN register until it is clear that the child's progress is no longer likely to give cause for concern

- **the child moves to stage 2:** if, after up to two review periods at stage 1, special help has not resulted in the child making satisfactory progress, the teacher or tutor and SEN coordinator may decide to move the child to stage 2.

2:84. As explained at paragraph 2:69 above, parents' evenings and similar occasions may allow parents to contribute to stage 1 reviews. Parents should always be told of the outcome and of any steps they can take to help their child at home. It is particularly important to talk with parents in person if the school is considering moving the child to stage 2.

Stage 2

2:85. At **stage 2** the SEN coordinator takes the lead in assessing the child's learning difficulty, and planning, monitoring and reviewing the special educational provision, working with the child's teachers and ensuring that the child's parents are consulted.

Trigger

2:86. The trigger for stage 2 is either a decision at a stage 1 review, or where, following discussions about an initial concern between teachers and parents, the SEN coordinator considers that early intensive action is necessary.

Roles and responsibilities

2:87. The school's SEN coordinator takes the lead in coordinating the child's special educational provision, consulting the child's teachers, who remain responsible for working with the child in the classroom.

Information required

2:88. At stage 2, the SEN coordinator and the child's class teacher or form/year tutor should review all the available information, including that gathered at stage 1. The SEN coordinator should also always seek information from health and social services and other agencies closely involved with the child:

from the school doctor or the child's general practitioner (with the consent of the parents)

- **medical advice**

from the social services and/or the education welfare service, as appropriate, on

- **any arrangements under an education supervision order (see Glossary)**
- **social services involvement with the child or the family**
- **any concerns about the child's welfare**
- **whether the local authority has the child on the Child Protection Register (see Glossary) or has any responsibilities for the child under the Children Act.**

2:89. The SEN coordinator may also collect information from any other agencies which may be closely involved with the child, including any supplementary school or voluntary organisation that runs leisure activities that the child attends.

Assessing and meeting the child's special educational needs

2:90. The SEN coordinator, consulting the child's class teacher or tutor, should consider:

- **all available information, including new information gathered at stage 2**
- **report of any stage 1 reviews.**

2:91. On the basis of the information now available, the SEN coordinator will decide whether:

- **to seek further advice**

  and/or

- **to draw up an individual education plan.**

Seeking further advice

2:92. If the information gathered reveals an area of the child's development or performance which warrants more detailed investigation or further advice, the SEN coordinator should record:

- **what further advice is being sought**
- **arrangements for the child pending receipt of advice**
- **review arrangements.**

Making special educational provision at stage 2: the individual education plan

2:93. The SEN coordinator, working with the child's class teacher or form/year tutor and any relevant curriculum specialists, should ensure that an individual education plan is drawn up. So far as possible, the plan should build on the curriculum the child is following alongside fellow pupils and should make use of programmes, activities, materials and assessment techniques readily available to the child's teachers. The plan should usually be implemented, at least in part, in the normal classroom setting. The SEN coordinator should, therefore, ensure close liaison between all relevant teachers. The plan should set out:

Stage 2 – Individual Education Plan

- **nature of the child's learning difficulties**
- **action – the special educational provision**
    - **staff involved, including frequency of support**
    - **specific programmes/activities/materials/equipment**
- **help from parents at home**
- **targets to be achieved in a given time**
- **any pastoral care or medical requirements**
- **monitoring and assessment arrangements**
- **review arrangements and date.**

2:94. The child's parents should always be informed of the action that the school proposes to take and any help they can give to their child at home.

2:95. The SEN coordinator should set a review date, which might be within a term. The coordinator should agree with the child's teachers the arrangements for monitoring his or her progress until the review and should inform the child's parents about any special arrangements that will apply to their child and for how long.

Review

2:96. The SEN coordinator should normally conduct the review, in consultation with the child's class teacher or form/year tutor and, where possible, parents. The review should focus on:

- **progress made by the child**
- **effectiveness of the education plan**
- **contribution made by parents at home**
- **updated information and advice**
- **future action.**

2:97. The outcome of the review may be:

- **the child continues at stage 2:** if the child's progress has been at least satisfactory, a new individual education plan may be drawn up. This should set targets in the light of the experience of the first plan. If progress remains satisfactory after two review periods, the SEN coordinator may decide to increase gradually the period between reviews

- **the child reverts to stage 1 or no longer needs special help:** if the child's progress continues to be at least satisfactory within this framework of planning and review for at least two review periods, the SEN coordinator may decide that the child no longer needs special educational provision under stage 2. The child may then be recorded as having special educational needs at stage 1. If the special educational provision has been wholly successful, the child may no longer need special help but the SEN coordinator should retain the child's name on the SEN register until it is clear that the child's progress is no longer likely to give cause for concern

- **the child moves to stage 3:** if after up to two review periods at stage 2, the child's progress is not satisfactory, additional expertise should be sought and the child should move to stage 3.

2:98. Parents should be invited to contribute to stage 2 reviews. They should always be told the outcome. It is particularly important to talk with parents in person if the school is considering moving the child to stage 3.

Stage 3

2:99. At **stage 3**, the school calls upon external specialist support to help the pupil make progress.

Trigger

2:100. The trigger for stage 3 is either a decision at a stage 2 review, or where, following discussions about an initial concern between the SEN coordinator, teachers and parents, the SEN coordinator, having consulted the head teacher, considers that early intensive action with external support is immediately necessary.

Roles and responsibilities

2:101. At stage 3, the SEN coordinator continues to take a leading role, working closely with the child's teachers and sharing responsibilities for the child with external specialist services relevant to the child's needs. Such support will come from teachers in a learning or behaviour support service; peripatetic teachers (see Glossary), for example, teachers of the hearing or visually impaired; the educational psychology service; child health or child and adolescent mental health services; social services; and advisers or teachers with a knowledge of information technology for children with special educational needs. Arrangements for securing help from these services will be affected by local policies, with which the SEN coordinator should be familiar. LEAs should provide information to all schools in their area about the range of services available. Help will also be available from publications on information technology and special educational provision, for example those produced by the National Council for Educational Technology (see Glossary).

2:102. Paragraph 3:7 below recommends that LEAs should gather information from maintained schools about registered pupils who live in the LEA's area and who are at stage 3. To ensure that the LEA's records are up-to-date, the head teacher or SEN coordinator should tell the responsible LEA whenever a child moves to stage 3.

Information required

2:103. The SEN coordinator and the child's class teacher or form/year tutor will consider:

- **all information gathered by the school over stages 1 and 2**
- **reports of stage 2 reviews.**

Assessing and meeting the child's needs

2:104. The SEN coordinator should then call in an appropriate specialist from a support service. This specialist will be qualified and experienced in the particular area of the child's special educational needs. The school may turn to a range of professionals, such as those listed in paragraph 2:101. Educational psychologists will play a key role in helping the school assess the information collected and the action taken to date; plan stage 3 special educational provision; and review that provision.

2:105. On the basis of all the information and advice gathered and the views of the external specialist, the SEN coordinator will decide whether:

- **to seek further advice from other agencies**

    and/or

- **to draw up a new individual education plan, including the involvement of support services.**

2:106. Whatever course of action is decided, the child's parents should be informed, wherever possible in person.

2:107. If the SEN coordinator and the external specialist consider that the information gathered reveals an area of the child's development or performance which warrants more detailed investigation or further advice from outside professionals, the SEN coordinator should record:

- **what further advice is being sought**
- **arrangements for the child pending receipt of advice**
- **review arrangements.**

Making special educational provision at stage 3: individual education plan and specialist involvement

2:108. There will be a new individual education plan for the child, describing new strategies for supporting the child's progress and the monitoring and review arrangements. The plan should be developed with the help of outside specialists but should usually be implemented, at least in part, in the normal classroom setting. The SEN coordinator should ensure, therefore, close liaison between relevant teachers. The plan should set out:

Stage 3 – Individual Education Plan
- **nature of the child's learning difficulty**
- **action – the special educational provision**
  - **school staff involved, including frequency and timing of support**
  - **external specialists involved, including frequency and timing**
  - **specific programmes/activities/materials/equipment**
- **help from parents at home**
- **targets to be achieved in a given time**
- **any pastoral care or medical requirements**
- **monitoring and assessment arrangements**
- **review arrangements and date.**

2:109. The plan should ensure a coordinated cross-curricular and inter-disciplinary approach which takes due account of the child's previous difficulties.

2:110. The SEN coordinator, working with the child's class teacher or form/year tutor and any relevant curriculum specialists, and with the help of the external specialist, should ensure that the plan is drawn up. Together they should consider a range of different teaching approaches and appropriate equipment and teaching materials, including the use of information technology. The specialist may be involved in teaching the child directly; may act in an advisory capacity, supporting the class teacher or form/year tutor in implementing the plan; or may recommend additional specialist teaching support, provided for example, by SEN support services. In some instances medical treatment or better management in school based on medical advice, may considerably reduce the child's special educational needs. Medical advice may include advice from the school health service, the child's general practitioner and from therapists.

Targets

2:111. Specific targets should be set for all aspects of the education plan. There should be special assessment arrangements made for those targets. Some of that assessment may be conducted by outside specialists, for example, educational psychologists.

2:112. The child's parents should always be informed of the action the school proposes to take. The SEN coordinator should set a review date, which should normally be within a term. The coordinator should agree with the child's teachers and the external specialists involved the arrangements for monitoring the child's progress against the targets established in the plan and should inform the child's parents about any special arrangements that will apply to their child and for how long.

Review

2:113. The SEN coordinator should convene stage 3 review meetings. The first review should focus on:

- **progress made by the child**
- **effectiveness of the education plan**
- **updated information and advice**
- **future action**
- **whether the child is likely in future to be referred for statutory assessment.**

2:114. At the review, external specialists should consider whether the analysis of the child by the school and the subsequent action is appropriate, and offer relevant advice. Other specialists may need to be brought in as a consequence of that advice.

2:115. The outcome of the review may be:

- **the child continues at stage 3:** if the child's progress has been at least satisfactory, a new individual education plan may be drawn up. This should set new targets in the light of the experience of the first plan. If progress remains satisfactory after two review periods, the SEN coordinator, consulting the head teacher and the external specialists involved, may decide to increase gradually the period between reviews

- **the child reverts to stage 1 or 2:** if a child's progress continues to be at least satisfactory within this framework of planning and review for at least two review periods, the SEN coordinator, consulting the head teacher and external specialists, may decide that the child no longer needs external specialist intervention and special educational provision under stage 3. The child may then be recorded as having special educational needs at stages 1 or 2, and action appropriate to those stages should be taken

— **the head teacher considers referring the child to the LEA for statutory assessment:** if, by the second stage 3 review, the child's progress is not satisfactory, the head teacher, on the advice of the SEN coordinator, should consider advising the LEA that a statutory assessment might be necessary. Any such approach should have the endorsement of the 'responsible person' – see paragraph 2:9.

2:116. Parents should always be invited to and encouraged to attend stage 3 reviews. They should also always be told the outcome. Where there is any question of the child being referred to the LEA for a statutory assessment, parents should always be consulted in person. By the time the head teacher considers referring the child for statutory assessment, there should be:

written information on

- **educational and other assessments, for example from an advisory specialist support teacher or an educational psychologist**
- **views of the parents and of the child**
- **the child's health**
- **social services' or education welfare service's involvement**

written evidence of

- **the school's action under the three stages**
- **education plans for the child**
- **regular reviews and their outcomes**
- **involvement of other professionals.**

2:117. Where a school refers a child for statutory assessment the head teacher may, by regulations made under section 19 of the 1988 Education Reform Act, give a special direction either modifying or disapplying (see Glossary) the National Curriculum for the child for a period of up to six months. Given the right of all pupils to the maximum possible access to the National Curriculum and the flexibility of that Curriculum, such exceptions should be very rare. Head teachers should not prejudge the outcome of any statutory assessment and should bear in mind that it may be more difficult to carry out an assessment if the child has been excepted from aspects of the National Curriculum. When the LEA are considering whether to make a statutory assessment or are conducting an assessment, the school, working in partnership with the child's parents and support services, remains responsible for the child's education, including his or her special educational provision.

2:118. The information on the child's learning difficulty and the evidence of the special educational provision made at stages 1-3 will form the basis of the LEA's consideration at stage 4 as to whether a statutory assessment is necessary. If the LEA's support services and, in particular, the LEA's educational psychologists have been involved in assessing the child and reviewing provision at stage 3, the LEA will be able to decide quickly whether a statutory assessment is necessary.

Summary

2:119. In summary, schools should adopt a staged response to children's special educational needs and:

- **employ clear procedures to identify and register children whose academic, physical, social or emotional development is giving cause for concern**

- **identify children's areas of weakness which require extra attention from their teachers or other members of staff**

- **develop, monitor, review and record, in consultation with parents and involving the child as far as possible, individual education plans designed to meet each child's identified needs. Such plans should include written information about:**
  - **individual programmes of work**
  - **performance targets**
  - **review dates, findings and decisions**
  - **parental involvement in and support for the plans**
  - **arrangements for the involvement of the child**
  - **information on any external advice or support**

- **assess children's performance, identifying strengths as well as weaknesses, using appropriate measures so that the rate of progress resulting from special educational provision can be assessed**

- **call upon specialist advice from outside the school to inform the school's strategies to meet the child's special educational needs in particular, but not necessarily only, at stage 3.**

2:120. The action involved in the staged model described in this Code is summarised in the following charts. As explained above, the procedures adopted by individual schools may vary according to their particular circumstances and the practice they follow in the light of this Code:

SCHOOL-BASED STAGES: STAGE 1

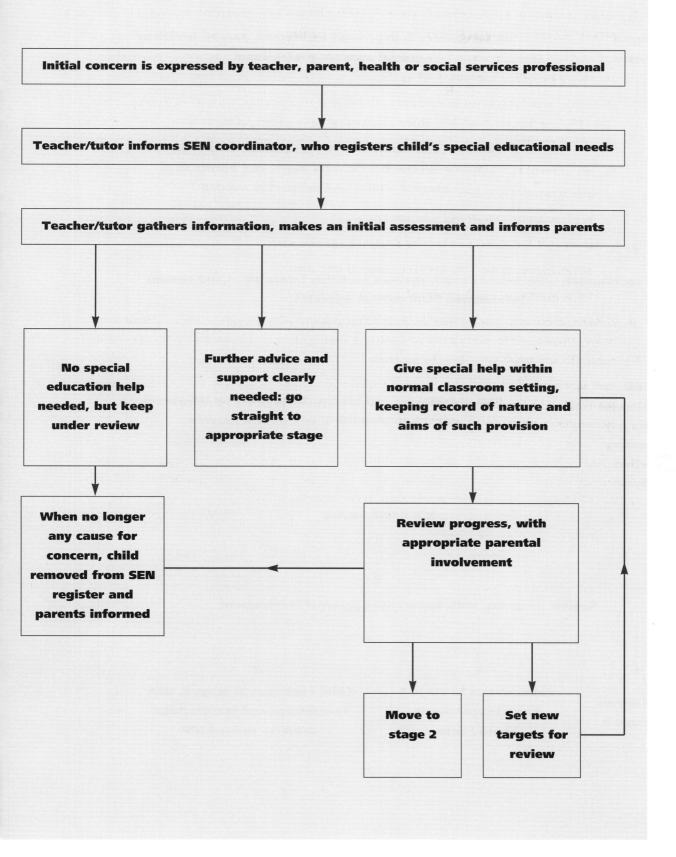

Initial concern is expressed by teacher, parent, health or social services professional

Teacher/tutor informs SEN coordinator, who registers child's special educational needs

Teacher/tutor gathers information, makes an initial assessment and informs parents

No special education help needed, but keep under review

Further advice and support clearly needed: go straight to appropriate stage

Give special help within normal classroom setting, keeping record of nature and aims of such provision

When no longer any cause for concern, child removed from SEN register and parents informed

Review progress, with appropriate parental involvement

Move to stage 2

Set new targets for review

SCHOOL-BASED STAGES: STAGE 2

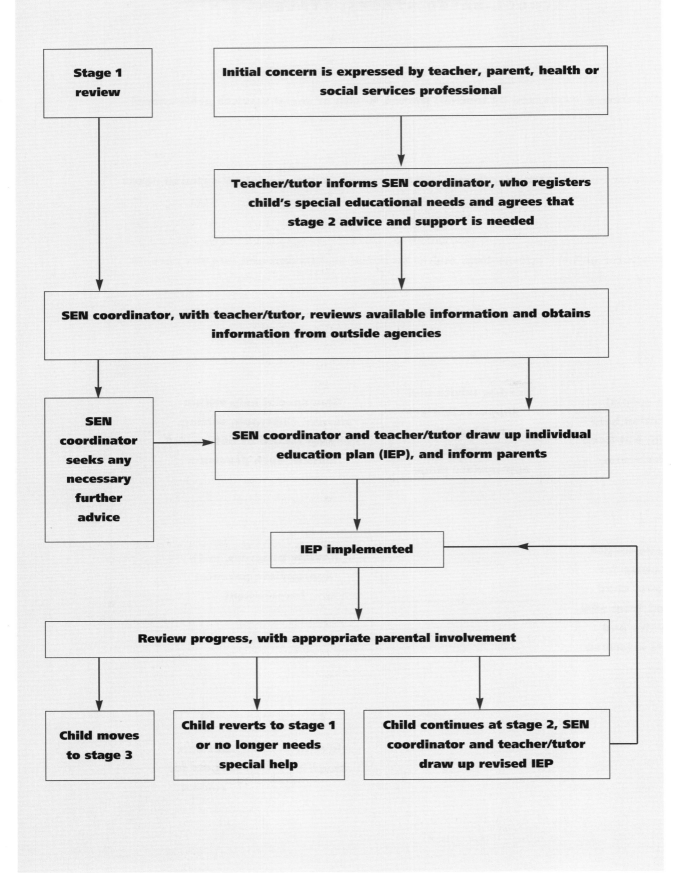

Stage 1 review

Initial concern is expressed by teacher, parent, health or social services professional

Teacher/tutor informs SEN coordinator, who registers child's special educational needs and agrees that stage 2 advice and support is needed

SEN coordinator, with teacher/tutor, reviews available information and obtains information from outside agencies

SEN coordinator seeks any necessary further advice

SEN coordinator and teacher/tutor draw up individual education plan (IEP), and inform parents

IEP implemented

Review progress, with appropriate parental involvement

Child moves to stage 3

Child reverts to stage 1 or no longer needs special help

Child continues at stage 2, SEN coordinator and teacher/tutor draw up revised IEP

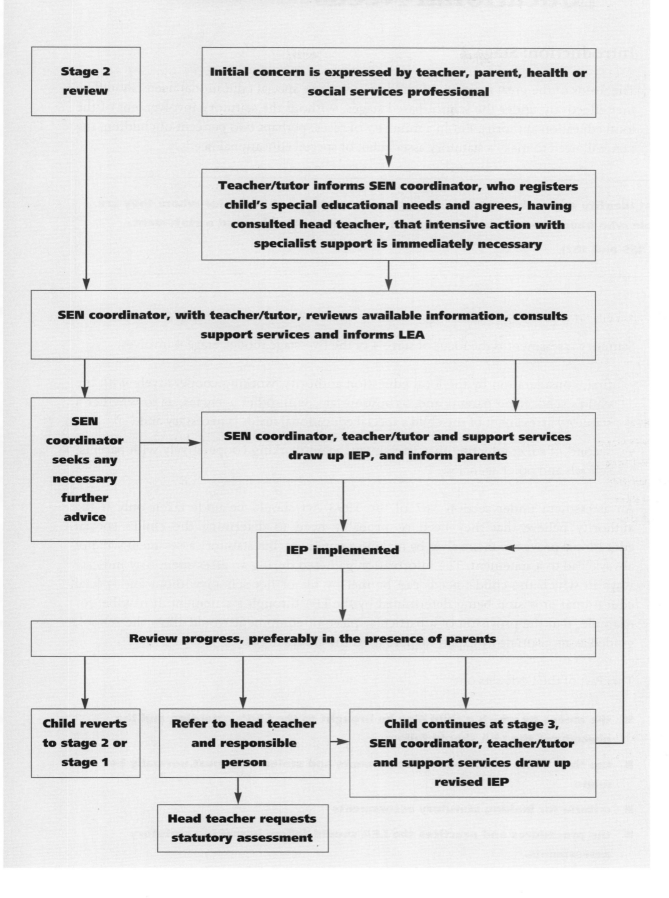

3. Statutory Assessment of Special Educational Needs

Introduction: Stage 4

3:1. The needs of the great majority of children who have special educational needs should be met effectively under the school-based stages, without the statutory involvement of the local education authority. But in a minority of cases, perhaps two per cent of children, the LEA will need to make a statutory assessment of special educational needs.

LEAs must identify and make a statutory assessment of those children for whom they are responsible who have special educational needs and who probably need a statement.

(Sections 165 and 167)

3:2. Statutory assessment is the focus of stage 4 of the five-stage model. Stage 4 involves:

– first, consideration by the local education authority, working cooperatively with the child's school and parents and, as appropriate, with other agencies, as to whether a statutory assessment of the child's special educational needs is necessary and

– second, if so, conducting that assessment, again working cooperatively with parents, schools and other agencies.

3:3. An assessment under section 167 of the 1993 Act should be undertaken only if the authority believe that they need or probably need to determine the child's special educational provision themselves by making a statement. But statutory assessment will not always lead to a statement. The information gathered during an assessment may indicate ways in which the child's needs can be met by his or her school without any special educational provision being determined by the LEA through a statement. It may be, for example, that the provision of a particular piece of equipment would allow the school, guided as appropriate by expert help, to meet the child's needs.

3:4. This Part of the Code sets out:

■ **the means by which a child may be brought to the LEA's attention and the procedures the LEA should follow**

■ **the time limits within which assessments and statements must normally be made**

■ **criteria for making statutory assessments**

■ **the procedures and practices the LEA should follow in making statutory assessments.**

Routes for referral

3:5. A child will be brought to the LEA's attention as possibly requiring an assessment through:

- **referral by the child's school or another agency**
- **a formal request for an assessment from a parent, or**
- **a formal request from a GM school directed to admit a pupil under section 13 of the Act.**

It is important that all requests for assessment are considered as quickly as possible, regardless of the source of the referral.

Referral by the child's school or other agency

3:6. In some cases, schools will conclude, after they have taken action to meet the learning difficulties of a child, that the child's needs remain so substantial that they cannot be met effectively within the resources normally available to the school. Schools may therefore draw the child to the attention of the local education authority with a view to an assessment under the 1993 Act. In a very small minority of cases schools may consider that a statutory assessment is necessary, even though no action has been taken at stages 1, 2 and 3 – see paragraphs 3:24 and 3:25 below. Children may also be drawn to the LEA's attention by the health services and social services departments. This is particularly likely with children under five who are not yet attending school – see Part 5.

3:7. LEAs have a duty to identify among those children in their area with special educational needs for whom they are responsible, those for whom they must make statements. To help fulfil this duty, LEAs should gather information from maintained schools about registered pupils who live in the LEA's area and who have special educational needs at stage 3.

3:8. When making a referral for a statutory assessment, the school should state clearly the reasons for the referral and submit the following material:

- **information, including:**
  - **the recorded views of parents and, where appropriate, children on the earlier stages of assessment and any action and support to date**
  - **evidence of health checks, for example relevant information on medical advice to the school**
  - **when appropriate, evidence relating to social services involvement**
- **written individual education plans at stages 2 and 3 indicating the approaches adopted, the monitoring arrangements followed and the educational outcomes**
- **reviews of each individual education plan indicating decisions made as a result**
- **evidence of the involvement and views of professionals with relevant specialist knowledge and expertise outside the normal competence of the school.**

Notice of a proposal to make a statutory assessment

3:9. The LEA will then consider whether to issue, under section 167(1), a notice to the parents that the LEA propose to make an assessment.

Before making an assessment, the LEA must write to the child's parents to explain their proposal. The LEA must also inform the parents of the procedure to be followed in making an assessment; of the name of the officer of the authority from whom further information may be obtained; and of their right to make representations and submit written evidence within a given time limit, which must not be less than twenty-nine days.

(Section 167)

3:10. When issuing such a notice, the LEA must:

i. tell parents of their right to make representations and submit written evidence. The LEA must set a time limit, which must not be less than 29 days. The LEA should encourage parents to make representations and to submit evidence, pointing out the importance of their contribution. When parents make representations orally, the LEA should agree a written summary with the parents. The LEA may invite parents to indicate formally if they do not wish to make or add to representations, in order that the LEA can then immediately consider whether a statutory assessment is necessary

ii. tell parents the name of an officer of the LEA who liaises with the parents over all the arrangements relating to statutory assessment and the making of a statement. This person is often known as the **Named LEA Officer** (see Glossary)

iii. set out clearly for parents the procedures that they will follow during statutory assessment and the possible subsequent drawing up of a statement. The LEA should also explain the precise timing of each of the various stages within the overall six-month time limit; indicate ways in which parents can assist the LEA in meeting the time limits; and explain the exceptions to the time limits.

3:11. LEAs should also:

i. give parents information about sources of independent advice, such as local or national voluntary organisations and any local support group or parent partnership scheme, which may be able to help them consider what they feel about their child's needs and the type of provision they would prefer

ii. tell parents about the role of the **Named Person** (see Glossary). This is someone who is preferably independent of the LEA and who can give the parents information and advice about their child's special educational needs, supporting them in their discussions with the LEA. The LEA should explain the difference between the Named Person and the Named LEA Officer. If the LEA do eventually make a statement, they must, at that stage, write to the parents, confirming the identity of the Named Person – see paragraphs 4:70–4:73. But there can be advantage in the LEA and the parents considering the identity of the Named Person at the start of the assessment process. The Named Person, who may be from a parents' group or a voluntary organisation, can then attend meetings, help parents express their views effectively, and thereby encourage parental participation at all stages. The LEA might inform parents that a local parent partnership scheme or a voluntary organisation can help them choose their Named Person

iii. ask the parents whether they would like the LEA to consult anyone in addition to those whom the LEA must approach for educational, medical, psychological and social services advice, should the LEA decide to proceed with the statutory assessment. The LEA should list those whom they must consult. The LEA should tell parents that they may also present any private advice or opinions which they have obtained and that this advice will be taken into account

iv. give parents information about the full range of provision available in maintained mainstream and special schools within the LEA. The information should be available at the earliest possible stage so that parents have every opportunity to consider their child's future placement and arrange visits to particular schools. Thus, by the time they submit representations to the LEA or express a preference for a particular school, they can do so from an informed point of view. It will be in the LEA's best interests to facilitate this process wherever possible, but they should be careful not to preempt the parents' preference or any representations they may later make.

3:12. Assessment can be stressful for parents. The value of early information and support to parents cannot be over-emphasised. The better informed and the better supported parents are, the better they are able to contribute as partners to the assessment of their child. The less well informed and the less well supported they are, the more likely they are to be anxious and defensive and the greater is the potential for confrontation.

3:13. LEAs should present information to parents in a manner that is not intimidating and which encourages participation and open discussion. All the above information should, if possible, be available in the first language of the child's parents and LEAs may wish to consider taped or video-taped versions of the information for parents who may find the information more accessible in that form.

3:14. LEAs may wish to consider whether the letter informing the parents of the LEA's proposal to assess should be personally delivered, for example by an education welfare officer. Personal delivery, along with the information about assessment, can provide parents with an additional opportunity to ask any questions and seek further advice. At this stage, the LEA should also seek parents' consent to any medical examination and psychological assessment of their child during the making of a statutory assessment. This will save time if the LEA decide that they must make an assessment.

3:15. If the school and the parents have been working closely with each other, this will not be the first the parents know of the possibility of a statutory assessment. There should be only a very small number of instances in which a sudden change in the child's circumstances, for example resulting from an accident or a sudden acceleration of a degenerative condition, or if the child had just moved into the area, might mean that the letter announcing the LEA's proposal to assess was unexpected. Even in such extreme instances, the LEA should attempt to inform parents first, in a familiar setting, of the intention to make an assessment.

Notification to other agencies of a proposal to assess

3:16. When informing parents of the proposal to assess, the LEA must copy the proposal to:

> - **the local authority's social services department**
> - **the district health authority**
> - **the head teacher of the child's school.**
>
> **(Regulation 5(1))**

The LEA should address the copy of the proposal to the designated officers of the SSD and DHA and should also copy the proposal to their own educational psychology service and any other relevant agencies, such as the education welfare service, who might be asked for advice should the assessment proceed. LEAs are not at this point asking these agencies to provide advice, but alerting them to the possibility of a request for advice in the near future. Such notice will give the health service and other agencies the opportunity to collate records and consult others who might be involved in providing advice. Early action at this stage within the health service and social services departments will in effect serve to extend the time available to those agencies for gathering advice, and thus help them meet the statutory time limits.

A formal request from a parent

3:17. Under section 172 or 173 of the Act, parents may ask the LEA to conduct a statutory assessment. The LEA must comply with such a request, unless they have made a statutory assessment within six months of the date of the request or unless they conclude, upon examining all the available evidence, that a statutory assessment is not necessary.

3:18. If schools, external specialists, including LEA support and educational psychology services, and parents have been working in partnership at stage 3, the parental request for a statutory assessment will often have been discussed between them and should come as no surprise to the LEA. But a parental request for a statutory assessment may reflect dissatisfaction or disagreement with the action taken in the school-based stages. Whatever the background, the LEA must take all parental requests seriously and take action immediately.

> **An LEA is responsible for a pupil at an independent school if he or she lives in their area *and* has been placed in that school at the expense of the LEA or the Funding Authority *or* has been brought to the LEA's attention as having or probably having special educational needs. The LEA must identify any such children who require statements.**
>
> **Section 165(3)**

3:19. Where a child attends an independent school (see Glossary), a parental request for an assessment may be the first that an LEA hear about that child. The procedure they follow and the factors they consider in deciding whether to make an assessment should be the same, regardless of the type of school the child attends: the LEA will wish to investigate evidence provided by the child's school and parents as to his or her learning difficulties and evidence about action taken by the school to meet those difficulties. LEAs may find it helpful to inform independent schools in their area of their duty to identify children for whom they are responsible and who require statements of special educational needs; to tell those schools of the procedures they will adopt and of the information they would expect to be given; and to encourage those schools to give the LEA early notification of any child who may require a statutory assessment.

3:20. When a child is referred by a parental request for a statutory assessment, the LEA should not issue a notice that they propose to make an assessment under section 167(1). But the LEA should immediately contact the parents in order to:

- **investigate further the nature of their concern**

- **ascertain the degree of their involvement and agreement with the special educational provision which has been made for their child at school**

- **give them full details of the assessment process and the information set out at paragraphs 3:10 and 3:11 above.**

Where under section 172(2) or 173(1) a parent has asked the LEA to arrange an assessment, the LEA shall give notice in writing to the social services department, the district health authority and the head teacher of the child's school of the fact that the request has been made, and tell them what help the LEA are likely to request if they decide to make an assessment.

(Regulation 5(3))

3:21. The LEA must inform the child's head teacher that the parents have made a request for a statutory assessment and should also ask the school for written evidence about the child, in particular, for the school's assessment of the child's learning difficulty and the school's account of the special educational provision that has been made. At the same time, the LEA should notify the educational psychology service and any other bodies which might later be asked for advice, and must notify the designated medical officers of the district health authority and the social services department.

A formal request from a grant-maintained school

3:22. The governing body of a grant-maintained (GM) school which has been directed to admit a child under section 13 of the Act, may ask the LEA responsible for the child to conduct a statutory assessment. This power of direction under section 13 will be used very exceptionally: it can be used only if a child has been refused admission to, or has been permanently excluded from, every school which is a reasonable distance from the child's home and provides suitable education.

3:23. The GM school should consult the parents before asking the LEA to conduct a statutory assessment. On receipt of such a request, so long as no assessment has been made in the previous six months, the LEA must issue a notice to the child's parents under section 174(2) of the Act. That notice must give the parents the same information as the notice required under section 167(1) and the LEA should follow the same procedures, encouraging the parents to make representations and submit evidence. Those representations must be made and evidence submitted within a given time limit, which must not be less than 29 days. As with a notice issued under section 167(1), a notice issued under section 174(2) must be copied to the district health authority and the social services department and to the head teacher of the child's school.

Children who may need immediate referral for statutory assessment

3:24. In the great majority of cases, before any reference is made to the LEA for a statutory assessment, the school will have assessed a child's learning difficulties and will have made special educational provision to meet the child's needs in the context of their staged assessment model. However, in a very small minority of cases, children may demonstrate such significant difficulties that the school may consider it impossible or inappropriate to carry out in full their chosen assessment procedure. For example, the school's concerns may have led to further diagnostic assessment or examination which demonstrates that a child has a major sensory or other impairment which, without immediate specialist intervention beyond the capacity of the school, will lead to increased learning difficulties (see also 3:6).

3:25. Where there is agreement between the school, the child's parents and any relevant consultant or adviser about the child's need for further multi-disciplinary assessment or there is concern that any delay might further damage the child's development, the child may be referred immediately to the LEA for consideration for statutory assessment. It is in such circumstances that assessment and emergency placements may be appropriate – see paragraph 4:13 – 4:16.

3:26. The LEA must then decide whether or not to make an assessment under section 167. The LEA should react consistently to requests from parents and referrals from schools and others for assessments and should subsequently make open and objective judgments as to whether a statement should be issued. The LEA should reach decisions as quickly as thorough consideration of all the issues allows and always, subject to certain prescribed exceptions, within the statutory time limits. Those time limits govern each step in the process of making assessments and statements and are described in the next section of this Part of the Code.

Time Limits for Making Assessments and Statements

3:27. It is in the interests of all concerned that statutory assessments and statements are made in a timely manner. It is also important that each part of the process is conducted with all reasonable speed so that, should the LEA decide, having proposed to make an assessment, that they need not make that assessment, or having assessed the child, that they need not issue a proposed statement, the parents are informed as quickly as possible and appropriate alternative arrangements are made.

3:28. The Regulations therefore set the following time limits in which the various parts of the process of making statutory assessments and statements must normally be conducted:

Where an LEA serve a notice on the child's parent informing him or her that they propose to make an assessment under section 167, or receive a request for such an assessment by the parent, the LEA shall within six weeks of the date of service of the notice, or of receipt of the request, give notice to the parent of their decision whether or not to make an assessment.

(Regulation 11(1), (2) and (3))

Where under section 167(4) an LEA have given notice to the parent of their decision to make an assessment they shall complete that assessment within ten weeks of the date on which such notice was given.

(Regulation 11(5))

Where an LEA have made an assessment of the child's educational needs under section 167 they shall within two weeks of the date on which the assessment is completed either serve a copy of a proposed statement on the parent or give notice of their decision not to make a statement.

(Regulation 14(1))

Where an LEA have served a copy of a proposed statement on the parent they shall within eight weeks of the date on which the proposed statement is served serve a copy of the completed statement.

(Regulation 14(2))

3:29. The cumulative effect of these time limits is that the period from the receipt of a request for a statutory assessment or the issue of a notice to parents under section 167(1) or section 174(2) to the issue of the final copy of the statement should normally be no more than 26 weeks.

3:30. The timetable for the whole process is as follows:

—	**considering whether a statutory assessment is necessary:** the period **from** the issue of a notice under sections 167(1) or 174(2) or the receipt of a request for a statutory assessment from parents **to** the decision as to whether to make a statutory assessment must normallybe no more than:	**6 weeks**
6 —	**making the assessment:** the period **from** the LEA's decision to make a statutory assessment **to** the LEA's decision as to whether to make a statement must normally be no more than:	**10 weeks**
16 —	**drafting the proposed statement or note in lieu (see Glossary):** the period **from** the LEA's decision whether to make a statement **to** the issue of a proposed statement or of a notice of the LEA's decision not to make a statement, giving full reasons, preferably in the form of a note in lieu, must normally be no more than:	**2 weeks**
18 —	**finalising the statement:** the period **from** the issue of the proposed statement **to** the issue of the final copy of the statement must normally be no more than:	**8 weeks**
26		**Total 26 weeks**

Considering whether a statutory assessment is necessary

3:31. The first task for the LEA, having notified the parents that a statutory assessment might be necessary or having received a request from the parents for such an assessment, is to decide whether a statutory assessment must be made. The timetable is as follows:

i. LEA conclude that it may be necessary to make a statement. Under 167(1), the LEA must inform parents that they propose to make an assessment, giving parents at least **29 days** to make representations.

Within 6 *weeks* of issuing a notice under 167(1), the LEA must tell parents that they will or will not make a statutory assessment. The period within which parents may make representations is part of the 6 weeks.

ii. Parents under 172(2) or 173(1) formally request a statutory assessment.

Within 6 *weeks* of receiving the request, the LEA must tell parents that they will or will not make a statutory assessment.

iii. Governing body of GM school, directed under section 13 to admit a pupil, request under 174(1) statutory assessment. LEA must inform parents under 174(2) that they propose to make an assessment, giving parents at least **29 days** to make representations.

Within 6 *weeks* of serving the notice under section 174(2), the LEA must tell parents *and* the governing body that they will or will not make a statutory assessment. The period within which parents may make representations is part of the 6 weeks.

Making the assessment and the statement

3:32. Having decided that the statutory assessment must be made, the LEA must seek parental, educational, medical, psychological and social services advice. They must also seek any other advice they consider appropriate and, where reasonable, consult those whom the parents have named. They should do so immediately and should ask all concerned to respond within six weeks.

3:33. The health services and social services departments *must* normally respond within six weeks of the date of receiving the request. Some weeks earlier, the LEA will have notified the designated medical officer and the designated officer of the social services department of the possibility of an assessment and should have, at the same time, sought the parents' consent to their child being medically examined as part of any assessment.

3:34. The health services and social services departments are not obliged to respond within six weeks if they have had no relevant knowledge of the child concerned prior to their receipt of a copy of the LEA's notice to parents that they propose to make an assessment or the LEA's letter notifying the health services and the SSD that they have received a request for an assessment. In those circumstances, however, the health service and social services departments should make every effort to respond promptly. In most cases, the health services will have some knowledge of the child as a result of the child's school seeking medical advice at stages 1-3.

3:35. Having received all the advice, the LEA must decide whether they need to make a statement. They must make that decision within ten weeks of issuing the notice under section 167(4).

3:36. If the LEA decide that a statement is necessary, they must draft a proposed statement and send a copy to the child's parents within two weeks. If they decide that a statement is not necessary, they must notify parents of that decision, giving their reasons, preferably in the form of a note in lieu of the statement, also within two weeks. The period from the issue of the notice under 167(4) to the issue of a proposed statement or a note in lieu of a statement should therefore normally be no more than 12 weeks.

3:37. Normally, the LEA will receive all the necessary advice within six weeks of the issue of the notice under section 167(4). Then they have a further six weeks in which to send the parents documented evidence of the outcome of the assessment: they must decide whether to make a statement within four weeks; and send parents a proposed statement or their written reasons why they will not make a statement, preferably in the form of a note in lieu, within a further two weeks. In practice, particularly if the LEA write notes in lieu with the same care as they write statements, attaching all the advice they have received (see paragraphs 4:17 – 4:23), the decision as to whether to write a statement or a note in lieu will often involve preparing a draft which can then take either form, according to the result of the LEA's deliberations. Deciding whether to make a statement and recording the results of the decision will be part and parcel of the same process. The critical point is that the parents must normally receive written evidence of the outcome of the assessment within 12 weeks of the start of the statutory assessment.

3:38. On receipt of the proposed statement, parents have a right to state a preference for the maintained school their child should attend and to make representations to, and hold meetings with, the LEA. The LEA must normally issue the final statement within *eight weeks* of the issue of the proposed statement.

Exceptions to the time limits

3:39. The paragraphs above have described the time limits which LEAs, the health services and social services must normally meet. But there will be circumstances in which it is not reasonable to expect the bodies concerned to meet those limits. The regulations therefore prescribe exceptions to the time limits.

3:40. The exceptions to the six week time limit within which LEAs must tell parents whether they will or will not make a statutory assessment are:

a. where the LEA have requested advice from the head teacher of a school during a period beginning one week before the school closes for a continuous period of not less than four weeks and ending one week before it reopens

b. where the LEA are aware of exceptional personal circumstances affecting the child or his or her parents (for example, family bereavement) during the six week period

c. where the parents or the child are absent from the area of the authority for a continuous period of not less than four weeks.

(Regulation 11(4))

3:41. The exceptions to the ten week time limit within which LEAs must make an assessment are:

a. where subsequent to receiving full advice as requested by the LEA, further advice or reports are exceptionally needed

b. where the parents want to provide advice for an assessment more than six weeks after the date on which an LEA's request for advice was received

c. where the LEA issue a request for educational advice during a period beginning one week before the school closes for a continuous period of not less than four weeks and ending one week before it reopens

d. where the LEA have requested advice from the health services or a social services department who have not replied within six weeks

e. where the LEA are aware of exceptional personal circumstances affecting the child or his or her parents (for example, family bereavement) during the process of assessment

f. where the parents or the child are absent from the area of the authority for a continuous period of not less than four weeks

g. where the child fails to honour an appointment for an examination or test.

(Regulation 11(6))

3:42. The exceptions to the six week time limit within which the health services and social services departments must provide information are:

a. **where there are exceptional personal circumstances affecting the child or his or her parents (for example, family bereavement) during the process of assessment**

b. **where the parents or the child are absent from the area of the authority for a continuous period of not less than four weeks**

c. **where the child fails to keep an appointment for an examination or test**

d. **where the health services or social services departments have had no relevant knowledge of the child prior to receiving a copy of the LEA's proposal to make a statutory assessment, issued under section 167(1) or section 174(2), or the notice that the child's parents have requested an assessment, issued under regulation 5(3).**

(Regulation 11(8))

3:43. The exceptions to the eight week time limit for the making of a statement are:

a. **where there are exceptional personal circumstances affecting the child or his or her parents (for example, family bereavement) during the making of a statement**

b. **where the parents or the child are absent from the area of the authority for a continuous period of not less than four weeks**

c. **where the parents, having received a proposed statement, want to make representations about the content of the statement after the 15 day period allowed for**

d. **where the parents seek more than one meeting under paragraph 4 of schedule 10**

e. **where the LEA have sent a written request to the Secretary of State seeking his consent under section 189(5)(b) to the child being educated at an independent school which is not approved by him and such consent has not been received by the LEA within two weeks of the date on which the request was sent.**

(Regulation 14(4))

3:44. LEAs should always strive to ensure that any delay arising from the exceptions is kept to a minimum. As soon as the conditions which have led to an exception no longer apply, the LEA should endeavour to complete the process as quickly as possible. Any remaining components of the process must, of course, be completed within their prescribed periods, regardless of whether exceptions have delayed earlier components. For example, even if the making of an assessment is delayed, the LEA must still notify parents of the outcome within two weeks of making their decision and, if a statement is to be made, must complete the final statement within eight weeks, unless further exceptions apply.

3:45. In summary, the time limits for making assessments and statements are as follows:

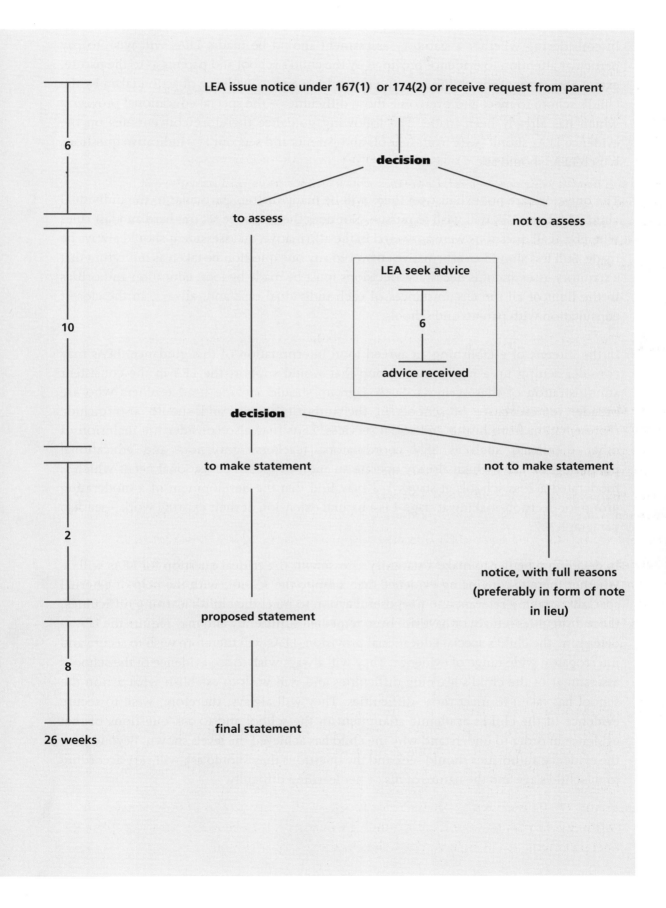

LEA issue notice under 167(1) or 174(2) or receive request from parent

decision

to assess   not to assess

LEA seek advice

6

advice received

decision

to make statement   not to make statement

proposed statement

notice, with full reasons (preferably in form of note in lieu)

final statement

6

10

2

8

26 weeks

Criteria for Deciding to Make a Statutory Assessment

3:46. In considering whether a statutory assessment should be made, LEAs will wish to pay particular attention to evidence provided by the child's school and parents as to the nature, extent and cause of the child's learning difficulties; and to evidence of action taken by the child's school to meet and overcome those difficulties – the special educational provision which has already been made. The following guidance therefore concentrates on the evidence LEAs should seek from schools and parents and sets out key indicative questions which LEAs should ask.

3:47. The questions are not exhaustive: there will be many matters particular to the individual child which the LEA will wish to pursue. Nor does the guidance set out hard and fast rules whereby, if all questions were answered in the affirmative, an assessment should always be made. Still less should an affirmative answer to any one question be taken as indicating that a statutory assessment is necessary. Decisions must be made by local education authorities in the light of all the circumstances of each individual case and, always, in the closest consultation with parents and schools.

3:48. In the interest of establishing an agreed local interpretation of this guidance, LEAs may consider setting up a moderating group that would support the LEA in the consistent administration of these criteria. Such a group should include head teachers who are broadly representative of schools in the authority's area, and should also include representation from health and social services. LEAs may also consider the inclusion of other members, such as SEN coordinators, teachers, governors and educational psychologists. LEAs which already operate an audit of special educational needs which is moderated across schools at stages 1-3 may find that the development of a moderating group for decision-making at stage 4 is a natural extension of their existing work – see also paragraph 4:7.

3:49. In deciding whether to make a statutory assessment, the critical question for LEAs will be whether there is convincing evidence that, despite the school, with the help of external specialists, taking relevant and purposeful action to meet the child's learning difficulties, those difficulties remain or have not been remedied sufficiently and may require the LEA to determine the child's special educational provision. LEAs will therefore wish to secure and interrogate a wide range of evidence. They will always wish to see evidence of the school's assessment of the child's learning difficulties and will wish to establish what action the school has taken to meet those difficulties. They will always, therefore, wish to secure evidence of the child's academic attainment in the school and to ask questions of that evidence in order to understand why the child has achieved the levels shown. Beyond that, the evidence authorities should seek and the questions they should ask will vary according to the child's age and the nature of his or her learning difficulty.

Academic attainment

3:50. LEAs will always require evidence of the child's academic attainment. Key indicators are provided by the results of assessments and tests in the core subjects of the National Curriculum. But the bare facts of academic attainment will not be sufficient in themselves for LEAs to conclude that a statutory assessment is or is not necessary. Those facts must always be understood in the context of the attainments of the child's peers, the child's progress over time and, where appropriate, expectations of the child's performance. A child's apparently weak performance may, on examination of the evidence, be attributable to factors in the school's organisation. Careful consideration of evidence of low attainment may reveal good progress from a low base. On the other hand, apparently satisfactory attainment may be found to fall far short of the performance expected of the child as assessed by his or her teachers, parents and others, including educational psychologists, who have observed the child closely, and, where appropriate, by standardised tests.

3:51. Nonetheless, academic attainment is the essential evidential starting point. LEAs should always be alert to evidence that a child's learning difficulties may be particularly complex or intractable. They should be alert, therefore, to significant discrepancies between:

i. a child's attainments in assessments and tests in core subjects of the National Curriculum and the attainment of the majority of children of his or her age

ii. a child's attainments in assessments and tests in core subjects of the National Curriculum and the performance expected of the child as indicated by a consensus among those who have taught and observed the child, including his or her parents, and supported by such standardised tests as can reliably be administered

iii. a child's attainment within one of the core subjects of the National Curriculum or between one core subject and another.

While National Curriculum assessments will therefore supply important evidence, LEAs should not delay their consideration of a child until such up-to-date assessment results are available. LEAs should also have regard to teachers' own recorded assessments of a child's classroom work, the outcome of individual education plans and any portfolio of the child's work compiled to illustrate his or her progress.

3:52. At the same time, LEAs should always seek evidence of identifiable non-academic factors affecting attainment. In all cases, LEAs should ask whether there is any evidence of:

i. problems with the child's health which may have led to recurrent or significant absences from school, or difficulty in concentrating or participating in the full range of curriculum activity while at school

ii. sensory impairment, for example hearing loss or visual problems

iii. speech and language difficulties

iv. poor school attendance

v. problems in the child's home circumstances

vi. any emotional and behavioural difficulties.

Special educational provision

3:53. The answers to these questions may indicate immediate remedies which would mean that a statutory assessment was not necessary. They might, on the other hand, suggest that a statutory assessment would help fully to identify the child's learning difficulties. In order to reach a decision, LEAs should examine and evaluate the action taken by the school to help the child: the special educational provision which has already been made. Therefore, except when the child's condition has changed suddenly, LEAs will normally wish to see clear recorded evidence of the learning difficulties identified and the action taken by the child's teachers at stage 1; the action taken by the SEN coordinator and teachers, and their evaluation at stage 2; and the action formulated, monitored and evaluated in conjunction with external specialists at stage 3. LEAs should also ask to see evidence that the school has made use of information from, and the insights of, parents and that, so far as possible, they have been involved in the process of meeting the child's learning difficulties. In cases where it is the parents who first express a concern to the school about the child's progress, the LEA should ask to see evidence that the school has investigated that concern thoroughly, in the same way as the school would have done if the child's teacher had expressed a concern. LEAs should also seek the medical advice which has been available to the school on the special educational needs of the child, and will wish to seek information from the child's parents as to any medical condition affecting the child's learning.

3:54. These considerations apply to all children referred to LEAs, by their parents or by their schools. But the precise nature of the evidence which LEAs should seek of the child's learning difficulty, its apparent cause and the special educational provision made by the school, will depend in some part on the nature of the child's learning difficulty or disability, and on his or her age. The following paragraphs therefore address the evidence which LEAs should seek and the questions they should ask about children with certain forms of learning difficulty or disability. There is a degree of repetition to enable each section to be read as a whole. This guidance does not assume that there are hard and fast categories of special educational need. It recognises, as LEAs will recognise, that each child is unique and that the questions asked by LEAs must reflect the particular circumstances of that child. It recognises, moreover, that children's learning difficulties may encompass more than one area of need. Nonetheless, parents, schools and LEAs should always be alive to the nature of the child's learning difficulty or disability, and should address the indicative questions which most closely fit the child's circumstances.

Learning difficulties

3:55. Some children with learning difficulties will be identified before school age and the great majority should be identified very early in their school careers. Their general level of academic attainment will be significantly below that of their peers. In most cases, they will have difficulty acquiring basic literacy and numeracy skills and many will have significant speech and language difficulties. Some may also have poor social skills and may show signs of emotional and behavioural difficulties.

3:56. Where children have severe or profound and multiple learning difficulties, the LEA will be able to draw upon a considerable body of existing knowledge arising from assessments and provision made by child health and social services, who may have been involved with children and families from a very early stage. Many children with severe or profound and multiple difficulties will have additional secondary disabilities, and assessment arrangements should take account of the possibility of such disabilities.

The child's learning difficulty

3:57. The LEA should seek clear recorded evidence of the child's academic attainment and ask, for example, whether:

i.   the child is not benefiting from working on programmes of study relevant to the Key Stage appropriate to his or her age, or is the subject of any temporary exception from the National Curriculum under section 19 of the Education Reform Act 1988

ii.   the child is working at a level significantly below that of his or her contemporaries in any of the core subjects of the National Curriculum – for example, under the current ten level graduation of achievement, an eight year old child who is working towards Level 1 or a 13-year old working at Level 2

iii.   there is evidence that the child is falling progressively behind the majority of children of his or her age in academic attainment in any of the National Curriculum core subjects as measured by National Curriculum assessments, other standardised tests and teachers' own recorded assessments of a child's classroom work, including any portfolio of the child's work

iv.   there is any evidence of impaired social interaction or communication or a significantly restricted repertoire of activities, interests and imaginative development

v.   there is evidence of significant problems in the child's home or family circumstances or in his or her school attendance record

vi.   there is evidence of significant emotional or behavioural difficulties, as indicated by clear recorded examples of withdrawn or disruptive behaviour; a marked and persistent inability to concentrate; difficulties in establishing and maintaining balanced relationships with his or her fellow pupils or with adults; and any other evidence of a significant delay in the development of life and social skills

vii.   there is any evidence of contributory or remediable medical problems or evidence from assessments or interventions by child health or social services. Information from such assessments and interventions will be particularly important in the case of children with severe or profound and multiple difficulties, whose needs are unlikely to be appropriately assessed without an interdisciplinary perspective.

The child's special educational provision

3:58. In the light of evidence about the child's learning difficulty, LEAs should consider the action taken by the school and, in particular, should ask whether:

i.   the school has, consulting outside specialists, formulated, monitored and regularly evaluated individual education plans, including structured literacy and/or numeracy support programmes, with clear targets; and the child's progress within such programmes, measured by criterion referenced or standardised tests, is significantly and consistently less than that which may be expected for the majority of children following such programmes

ii. the school has sought the views of and involved the child's parents at each stage

iii. the school has explored the possible benefits of, and where practicable secured access for the child to, appropriate information technology, for example word processing facilities, overlay keyboards and software, providing training in the use of that technology for the child, his or her parents and staff, so that the child is able to use that technology across the curriculum in school, and wherever appropriate, at home

iv. the school has implemented its policy on pastoral care and guidance and sought external advice to meet any social, emotional or behavioural difficulties

v.   the school has, with the parents' consent, notified and sought the assistance of the school doctor and/or the child's general practitioner, as appropriate.

3:59. Where the balance of evidence presented to and assessed by the LEA suggests that the child's learning difficulties:

—   are significant and/or complex

—   have not responded to relevant and purposeful measures taken by the school and external specialists, and

—   *may* call for special educational provision which cannot reasonably be provided within the resources normally available to mainstream schools in the area

the LEA should consider very carefully the case for a statutory assessment of the child's special educational needs.

Specific learning difficulties (for example Dyslexia)

3:60. Some children may have significant difficulties in reading, writing, spelling or manipulating number, which are not typical of their general level of performance. They may gain some skills in some subjects quickly and demonstrate a high level of ability orally, yet may encounter sustained difficulty in gaining literacy or numeracy skills. Such children can become severely frustrated and may also have emotional and/or behavioural difficulties.

The child's learning difficulty

3:61. The LEA should seek clear, recorded evidence of the child's academic attainment and ask, for example, whether:

i. there are extreme discrepancies between attainment in different core subjects of the National Curriculum or within one core subject, particularly English/Welsh. LEAs should be especially alert if there is evidence that, within the core subject of English/Welsh, a child has attained average or high levels in Attainment Target 1, speaking and listening (oral in Welsh), but significantly lower levels in AT2, reading, and/or AT3, writing

ii. expectations of the child, as indicated by a consensus among those who have taught and closely observed him or her, supported, as appropriate, by appropriately administered standardised tests of cognitive ability or oral comprehension, are significantly above his or her attainments in National Curriculum assessments and tests and/or the results of appropriately administered standardised reading, spelling or mathematics tests

iii. there is clear, recorded evidence of clumsiness; significant difficulties of sequencing or visual perception; deficiencies in working memory; or significant delays in language functioning

iv. there is evidence of problems sometimes associated with specific learning difficulties, such as severe emotional and behavioural difficulties, as indicated by clear, recorded examples of withdrawn or disruptive behaviour, an inability to concentrate, or signs that the child experiences considerable frustration or distress in relation to his or her learning difficulties. LEAs should be particularly alert if there is evidence of such difficulties in some classes or tasks such as reading or writing but not in others.

The child's special educational provision

3:62. In the light of evidence about the child's learning difficulty, the LEA should consider the action taken by the school and, in particular, should ask whether:

i. the school has taken action to make both the curriculum and the school day accessible to the child by alerting all teachers to the child's particular needs, helping the child develop appropriate practices for taking down and recording information, adopting appropriate marking policies and promoting the use of such devices as personal dictionaries

ii. the school has formulated, closely monitored and fully evaluated, in conjunction with external experts, individual education plans, including structured literacy programmes involving, for example:

– **for reading:** a reading programme structured to respond to the child's particular strengths and weaknesses as revealed by a diagnostic assessment of the child's reading performance, and including phonics teaching

– **for spelling:** a structured spelling support programme promoted and monitored by teachers across the curriculum, such as simultaneous oral spelling linked to the development of cursive writing

— **the use of multi-sensory teaching strategies:** directed to developing the basic skills of reading, spelling, or number

iii. the school, consulting external specialists, including educational psychologists, has monitored the child's progress as a result of the action taken and has clearly demonstrated through, for example, appropriately applied reading and spelling tests and teacher assessment, that the child has not made significant progress and/or that the child's level of attainment is falling further behind that of the majority of children

iv. the school has taken into account, investigated and recorded parental concern, and has sought to enrol the support of parents by involving them in creating, delivering and evaluating detailed plans to help their child in and out of school

v. the school has explored the possible benefits of, and where practicable secured access for the child to, appropriate information technology, for example word processing facilities including spell-checkers and other software, providing training in the use of that technology for the child, his or her parents and staff, so that the child is able to use that technology across the curriculum in school, and wherever appropriate, at home

vi. the school has closely monitored the child's emotional and behavioural responses to his or her learning difficulties and, if necessary, has provided help to reduce anxiety and enhance self-esteem

vii. the school has, with the parents' consent, notified and sought the assistance of the school doctor and/or the child's general practitioner, as appropriate.

3:63. Where the balance of evidence presented to and assessed by the LEA suggests that the child's learning difficulties:

— are significant and/or complex

— have not responded to relevant and purposeful measures taken by the school and external specialists, and

— *may* call for special educational provision which cannot reasonably be provided within the resources normally available to mainstream schools in the area

the LEA should consider very carefully the case for a statutory assessment of the child's special educational needs.

Emotional and behavioural difficulties (EBD)

3:64. Pupils with emotional and/or behavioural difficulties have learning difficulties as defined at paragraph 2:1 above. They may fail to meet expectations in school and in some but by no means all cases may also disrupt the education of others.

3:65. Emotional and behavioural difficulties may result, for example, from abuse or neglect; physical or mental illness; sensory or physical impairment; or psychological trauma. In some cases, emotional and behavioural difficulties may arise from or be exacerbated by circumstances within the school environment. They may also be associated with other learning difficulties. The causes and effects of EBD are discussed in more detail in the Circular: 'The Education of Children with Emotional and Behavioural Difficulties', where the concept of a continuum of difficulty is developed.

3:66. Emotional and behavioural difficulties may become apparent in a wide variety of forms – including withdrawn, depressive or suicidal attitudes; obsessional preoccupation with eating habits; school phobia; substance misuse; disruptive, anti-social and uncooperative behaviour; and frustration, anger and threat of or actual violence.

3:67. Teachers should always carefully record instances of behavioural disturbance, even when no apparent cause is evident. Advice on observation and recording is also given in the Circular: 'The Education of Children with Emotional and Behavioural Difficulties'.

The child's learning difficulty

3:68. The LEA should seek clear, recorded evidence of both the child's academic attainment and the nature of his or her emotional and behavioural difficulties, asking, for example, whether:

i. there is a significant discrepancy between, on the one hand, the child's cognitive ability and expectations of the child as assessed by his or her teachers, parents and others directly concerned, supported, as appropriate, by appropriately administered standardised tests and, on the other hand, the child's academic attainment as measured by National Curriculum assessments and teachers' own recorded assessments of the child's classroom work, including any portfolio of the child's work compiled to illustrate his or her progress

ii. the child is unusually withdrawn, lacks confidence and is unable to form purposeful and lasting relationships with peers and adults: the LEA will look for clear, detailed evidence from the school and external specialists based on close observation of the child

iii. there is evidence of severely impaired social interaction or communication, or a significantly restricted repertoire of activities, interests and imaginative development

iv. the child attends school irregularly: the LEA will wish to establish whether there is any pattern to or cause of the child's non-attendance

v. there is clear, recorded evidence of any obsessional eating habits

vi. there is clear, recorded evidence of any substance or alcohol misuse

vii. the child displays unpredictable, bizarre, obsessive, violent or severely disruptive behaviour. The LEA will wish to establish whether there is any pattern to such behaviour, for example whether it is confined to a particular class, teacher, task or given set of circumstances, and will seek clear examples in the form of specific, recorded instances over a period of time, usually not less than a term

viii. the child has participated in or has been subject to bullying at school; has been subject to neglect and/or abuse at home; and/or has faced major difficulties at home: again, the LEA will seek clear, recorded evidence

ix. there is any suggestion that the child may have a significant mental or physical health problem: the LEA should be alert to any sudden unpredictable changes in the child's behaviour which have no obvious cause, but which might indicate a developing neurological impairment, epilepsy, or another physical cause.

The child's special educational provision

3:69. In the light of this evidence, the LEA should consider the action taken by the school and others to meet the child's needs and, in particular, will wish to ask whether:

i. the school has sought appropriate external advice and then, following thorough discussions with the child, has formulated, implemented, monitored and evaluated individual education plans, including a behaviour management programme

ii. the school has followed, as appropriate in the individual case, the provisions of its policies on behaviour and on pastoral care and guidance

iii. all staff have been fully informed of the child's difficulties and a consistent approach to remedying these difficulties has been taken across the school

iv. the school has sought a constructive relationship with the child's parents/carers, encouraging them to participate in their child's education, including visiting the school on a regular basis

v. the school has, where appropriate, notified and sought the involvement of the education welfare service and/or the social services department

vi. the school has explored the possible benefits of, and where practicable secured access for the child to, appropriate information technology as a means of motivating and stimulating the child, for example word processing facilities, painting programs and other software which encourages communication and self-expression, providing training in the use of that technology for the child, his or her parents and staff, so that the child is able to use that technology across the curriculum in school, and wherever appropriate, at home

vii. the school has, with the parents' consent, notified and sought the assistance of the school doctor and/or the child's general practitioner, as appropriate.

3:70. Where the balance of evidence presented to and assessed by the LEA suggests that the child's emotional and behavioural difficulties:

– are significant and/or complex

– have not responded to relevant and purposeful measures taken by the school and external specialists, and

– may call for special educational provision which cannot reasonably be provided within the resources normally available to mainstream schools in the area

the LEA should consider very carefully the case for a statutory assessment of the child's special educational needs.

Physical disabilities

3:71. A child's physical disabilities may be the result of an illness or injury, which might have short or long-term consequences, or may arise from a congenital condition. Such difficulties may, without action by the school or the LEA, limit the child's access to the full curriculum. Some children with physical disabilities may also have sensory impairments, neurological problems and learning difficulties.

The child's learning difficulty/disability

3:72. The LEA should seek clear, recorded evidence of both the child's academic attainment and the nature of his or her physical disability, asking, for example, whether:

i. there is a significant discrepancy between the child's attainment, as measured by National Curriculum assessments and tests and teachers' own recorded assessments of a child's classroom work, including any portfolio of the child's work, and the attainments of the majority of children of his or her age

ii. there is a significant discrepancy between expectations of the child as assessed by the child's teachers, parents and external specialists who have closely observed him or her, supported, as appropriate, by the results of standardised tests of cognitive ability, and the child's attainment as measured by National Curriculum assessments and tests

iii. the child is unable fully to take part in particular aspects of the school's curriculum without close adult supervision and/or substantial adaptation of teaching materials or the environment

iv. the child has significant self-help difficulties in, for example, dressing, toileting or feeding and/or the child's condition gives rise to serious safety issues

v. there is clear substantiated evidence based on specific examples that the child's inability fully to take part in school life places the child under significant emotional or physical stress.

The child's special educational provision

3:73. In the light of evidence about the child's academic attainments and physical disability, the LEA should consider the action taken by the school and, in particular, should ask whether:

i. the school, consulting the LEA's support services and, where appropriate, regional organisations expert in information technology for communication difficulties (see Glossary), has explored the possible benefits of, and where practicable secured access for the child to, appropriate information technology, for example special keyboards and switch input to allow access to word processing facilities and software, providing training in the use of that technology for the child, his or her parents and staff, so that the child is able to use that technology across the curriculum in school, and wherever appropriate, at home

ii. the school has formulated, implemented, monitored and evaluated individual education plans to support full access to the curriculum and has given consideration, for example, to the child's space requirements in the classroom and such matters as the storage and maintenance of equipment

iii. the school has fully applied the access provisions of its SEN policy in the case of the individual child concerned and has taken all reasonable steps to improve access to independent learning and the physical environment of the school for the child, seeking external advice on basic adaptations from, for example, the LEA, the local authority's social services department, health and safety experts and voluntary organisations

iv. the school has, with the parents' consent, notified and sought the assistance of the school doctor and/or the child's general practitioner as appropriate.

3:74. Where the balance of the evidence presented to and assessed by the LEA suggests that the child's learning difficulties and/or disabilities:

– are significant and/or complex

– have not been met by relevant and purposeful measures taken by the school and external specialists, and

– may call for special educational provision which cannot reasonably be provided within the resources normally available to mainstream schools in the area

the LEA should consider very carefully the case for a statutory assessment of the child's special educational needs.

Sensory impairments: hearing difficulties

3:75. A significant proportion of children has some degree of hearing difficulty. Hearing losses may be temporary or permanent. Temporary hearing losses are usually caused by the condition known as 'glue ear' and occur most often in the early years. Such hearing losses fluctuate and may be mild or moderate in degree. They can seriously compound other learning difficulties. Schools should be alert to such evidence as persistently discharging ears.

3:76. Permanent hearing losses are usually sensori-neural and vary from mild through moderate, to severe or profound. Children with severe or profound hearing loss may have severe or complex communication difficulties.

3:77. Early recognition, diagnosis and treatment, and specialist support for pupils with hearing difficulties, are essential to ensure the child's language acquisition, academic achievement and emotional development do not suffer unnecessarily.

The child's learning difficulty/disability

3:78. The LEA should seek clear recorded evidence of both the child's academic attainment and the extent and nature of his or her hearing difficulty, asking, for example, whether:

i.   there is a significant discrepancy between the child's attainment, as measured by National Curriculum assessments and tests, and teachers' own recorded assessments of a child's classroom work, including any portfolio of the child's work, and the attainment of the majority of children of his or her age

ii. there is a significant discrepancy between the expectations of the child as assessed by the child's teachers, parents and external specialists who have closely observed the child, supported, as appropriate, by the results of standardised tests of cognitive ability, and the child's attainment as measured by National Curriculum assessments and tests

iii. there is clear recorded evidence of the extent and nature of the child's hearing loss in the form of the results of any recent audiometric assessments, with relevant audiograms

iv. there is clear recorded evidence that the child's hearing difficulty significantly impairs his or her emotional or social development, access to the curriculum, ability to take part in particular classroom activities or participation in aspects of school life

v.   there is clear substantiated evidence, based on specific examples, that the child's hearing difficulty places the child under stress, with associated withdrawn or frustrated behaviour.

The child's special educational provision

3:79. In the light of evidence about the child's academic attainment and hearing difficulty, the LEA should consider the action taken by the school and, in particular, should ask whether:

i.   the school has taken the advice of appropriate external specialists, including, for example, qualified teachers of the deaf, the LEA's support services and voluntary bodies

ii. the school has formulated, implemented, monitored and evaluated individual education plans to support full access to and active involvement in the curriculum and the school's life, addressing such matters as the child's positioning in the class, the scope for paired activities with hearing children or adults and the use of hearing aids and other relevant equipment

iii. all teachers and adults in the school have been alerted to the child's hearing difficulty and are aware of basic measures they should take to overcome or circumvent that difficulty

iv. the school has sought the views of, and involved, the child's parents at each stage

v.   the school has explored the possible benefits of, and where practicable secured access for the child to, appropriate information technology, for example word processing facilities, painting programs and other software which uses the visual power of the computer, providing training in the use of that technology for the child, his or her parents and staff, so that the child is able to use that technology across the curriculum in school, and wherever appropriate, at home

vi. the school has, with the parents' consent, notified and sought the assistance of the school doctor and/or the child's general practitioner, as appropriate.

80. Where the balance of the evidence presented to and assessed by the LEA suggests that the child's learning difficulties and/or disabilities:

- are significant and/or complex

- have not been met by relevant and purposeful measures taken by the school and external specialists, and

- may call for special educational provision which cannot reasonably be provided within the resources normally available to mainstream schools in the area

the LEA should consider very carefully the case for a statutory assessment of the child's special educational needs.

Sensory impairment: visual difficulties

3:81. Visual difficulties take many forms with widely differing implications for a child's education. They range from relatively minor and remediable conditions to total blindness. Some children are born blind; others lose their sight, partially or completely, as a result of accidents or illness. In some cases visual impairment is one aspect of multiple disability. Whatever the cause of the child's visual impairment, the major issue in identifying and assessing the child's special educational needs will relate to the degree and nature of functional vision, partial sight or blindness, and the child's ability to adapt socially and psychologically as well as to progress in an educational context.

The child's learning difficulty/disability

3:82. The LEA should seek clear recorded evidence of both the child's academic attainment and the nature of his or her visual difficulty, asking, for example, whether:

i. there is a significant discrepancy between the child's attainment, as measured by National Curriculum assessments and tests, and teachers' own recorded assessments of a child's classroom work, including any portfolio of the child's work, and the attainment of the majority of children of his or her age

ii. there is a significant discrepancy between the expectations of the child as assessed by the child's teachers, parents and external specialists who have closely observed the child, supported, as appropriate, by the results of standardised tests of cognitive ability, and the child's attainment as measured by National Curriculum assessments and tests

iii. there is clear recorded evidence of the extent of the child's visual difficulty, in the form of assessments of the level of the child's functional vision

iv. there is clear recorded evidence that the child's visual difficulty significantly impairs his or her mobility, emotional or social development, access to the curriculum, ability to take part in particular classroom activities or participation in aspects of school life

v.   there is clear substantiated evidence, based on specific examples, that the child's visual difficulty places the child under stress, with associated withdrawn or frustrated behaviour.

The child's special educational provision

3:83.   In the light of evidence about the child's academic attainments and visual disability, the LEA should consider the action taken by the school and, in particular, should ask whether:

i.   the school has taken the advice of appropriate external specialists, including, for example, a qualified teacher of the visually impaired, a mobility officer qualified to work with visually impaired children, the LEA's support services or a voluntary body

ii.   the school has formulated, implemented, monitored and evaluated individual education plans to support full access to and involvement in the curriculum and school life, ensuring that all teachers are aware of the child's difficulty and adopting appropriate classroom management measures

iii.   the school has fully applied the access provisions of its SEN policy in the case of the individual child and, seeking external advice as appropriate, has explored the scope for and followed recommendations regarding physical adaptations – for example in the use of handrails, or in lighting and contrast application and training – to support the child's mobility

iv.   the school has, in consultation with external specialists, for example the LEA's support services and/or voluntary organisations, explored the possible benefits of, and where practicable secured access for the child to, appropriate information technology, for example voice synthesizers linked to computers, providing training in the use of that technology for the child, his or her parents and staff, so that the child is able to use that technology across the curriculum in school, and wherever appropriate, at home

v.   the school has sought the views of, and involved, the child's parents at each stage

vi.   the school has, with the parents' consent, notified and sought the assistance of the school doctor and/or the child's general practitioner, as appropriate.

3:84.   Where the balance of the evidence presented to and assessed by the LEA suggests that the child's learning difficulties and/or disabilities:

–   are significant and/or complex

–   have not been met by relevant and purposeful measures taken by the school and external specialists and

–   may call for special educational provision which cannot reasonably be provided within the resources normally available to mainstream schools in the area

the LEA should consider very carefully the case for a statutory assessment of the child's special educational needs.

Speech and language difficulties

3:85. Although most speech and language difficulties will have been identified before a child reaches school, some children will still have significant speech and language difficulties which impair their ability to participate in the classroom by the time they start school. This may in turn have serious consequences for the child's academic attainment and also give rise to emotional and behavioural difficulties. The early identification of such speech and language difficulties and prompt remedial action are therefore essential.

The child's learning difficulty/disability

3:86. The LEA should seek clear recorded evidence of both the child's academic attainment and the nature of his or her communication difficulty, asking, for example, whether:

i. there is a significant discrepancy between the child's attainment, as measured by National Curriculum assessments and tests, and teachers' own recorded assessments of a child's classroom work, including any portfolio of the child's work, and the attainment of the majority of children of his or her age

ii. there is a significant discrepancy between the expectations of the child as assessed by the child's teachers, parents and external specialists who have closely observed the child, supported, as appropriate, by the results of standardised tests of cognitive ability, and the child's attainment as measured by National Curriculum assessments and tests

iii. the child's expressive and/or receptive language development is significantly below that of the majority of children of his or her age as measured by a standardised language assessment test, or there is a major discrepancy between the child's expressive and receptive levels of functioning

iv. there is clear substantiated evidence, based on specific examples, that the child's communication difficulties impede the development of purposeful relationships with adults and/or fellow pupils and/or give rise to other emotional and behavioural difficulties

v. there is any evidence of a hearing impairment which may coexist with, or cause, the speech and language difficulty.

The child's special educational provision

3:87. In the light of evidence about the child's academic attainment and communication difficulties, the LEA should consider the action taken by the school and, in particular, should ask whether:

i. the school has, with the parents' consent, sought the advice of the school doctor and/or the child's general practitioner, as appropriate, and of a speech and language therapist and other external specialists, for example a language development advisory teacher, and has, together with the child's parents and involving all teachers concerned with the child, implemented, monitored and evaluated individual education plans for the child to support full access to, and involvement in, the school and social life

ii. the school has closely monitored the child's emotional and behavioural condition and, if necessary, has provided pastoral help to reduce anxiety and enhance self-esteem

iii. the school has, consulting the LEA's support services and, where appropriate, regional organisations expert in information technology for communication difficulties (see Glossary), explored the possible benefits of, and where practicable secured access for the child to, appropriate information technology, for example word processing facilities, painting programs and software which encourages communication and self-expression, providing training in the use of that technology for the child, his or her parents and staff, so that the child is able to use that technology across the curriculum in school, and wherever appropriate, at home.

3:88. Where the balance of the evidence presented to and assessed by the LEA suggests that the child's learning difficulties and/or disabilities:

— are significant and/or complex

— have not been met by relevant and purposeful measures taken by the school and external specialists and

— may call for special educational provision which cannot reasonably be provided within the resources normally available to mainstream schools in the area

the LEA should consider very carefully the case for a statutory assessment of the child's special educational needs.

Medical conditions

3:89. Some medical conditions may, if appropriate action is not taken, have a significant impact on the child's academic attainment and/or may give rise to emotional and behavioural difficulties. Some of the commonest medical conditions are likely to be congenital heart disease, epilepsy, asthma, cystic fibrosis, haemophilia, sickle cell anaemia, diabetes, renal failure, eczema, rheumatoid disorders, and leukaemia and childhood cancers.

3:90. These conditions may in themselves significantly impair the child's ability to participate fully in the curriculum and the wider range of activities in the school. Some medical conditions will affect the child's progress and performance intermittently, others on a continuous basis throughout the child's school career. Drug therapies, such as those required for the treatment of leukaemia and childhood cancers, may compound the problems of the condition and have implications for the child's education. The medication required for the control of epilepsy may similarly impair concentration and cause difficulties in the classroom. In some instances, children and young people with potentially life-threatening conditions such as cystic fibrosis or heart disease may have periods of hospitalisation and emotional and behavioural difficulties related to their conditions and the associated restrictions on everyday living and the nature of the treatment required.

3:91. Consultation and open discussion between the child's parents, the school, the school doctor or the child's general practitioner, the community paediatrician and any specialist

services providing treatment for the child will be essential to ensure that the child achieves maximum progress and also that the child is not unnecessarily excluded from any part of the curriculum or school activity because of anxiety about his or her care and treatment. See also the Circular: 'The Education of Sick Children'.

The child's learning difficulty

3:92. The LEA should seek clear recorded evidence of both the child's academic attainment and the nature of his or her medical condition, asking, for example, whether:

i. there is a significant discrepancy between the child's attainment, as measured by National Curriculum assessments and tests, and teachers' own recorded assessments of a child's classroom work, including any portfolio of the child's work, and the attainment of the majority of children of his or her age

ii. there is a significant discrepancy between the expectations of the child as assessed by the child's teachers, parents and external specialists who have closely observed the child, supported, as appropriate, by the results of standardised tests of cognitive ability, and the child's attainment as measured by National Curriculum assessments and tests

iii. there is clear recorded evidence that the child's medical condition significantly impedes or disrupts his or her access to the curriculum, ability to take part in particular classroom activities or participation in aspects of school life

iv. there is clear substantiated evidence, based on specific examples, that the child's medical condition has given rise to emotional or behavioural difficulties

v. there is evidence of significant and recurrent absences from school.

The child's special educational provision

3:93. In the light of evidence about the child's academic attainment and medical condition, the LEA should consider the action taken by the school and, in particular, should ask whether:

i. the school has, with the parents' consent, notified and sought the assistance of the school doctor, the child's general practitioner or any specialist child health service, as appropriate

ii. all staff have been fully informed of the child's medical condition and a consistent approach to managing the child's education has been taken across the school

iii. the school has sought the views of, and involved, the child's parents at each stage

iv. the school has sought the cooperation of those within the local education authority responsible for the education of children who are at home and, as appropriate, in hospital, as a result of illness.

3:94. Where the balance of the evidence presented to and assessed by the LEA suggests that the child's learning difficulties and/or disabilities:

– are significant and/or complex

- have not been met by relevant and purposeful measures taken by the school and external specialists, and

- may call for special educational provision which cannot reasonably be provided within the resources normally available to mainstream schools in the area

the LEA should consider very carefully the case for a statutory assessment of the child's special educational needs.

The Conduct of Statutory Assessment

> **Where under section 167(1) or 174(2) the LEA serve a notice on the child's parent informing him or her that they propose to make an assessment under section 167, they shall within six weeks of serving that notice give notice to the child's parent under section 167(4) or 174(5) of their decision to make an assessment, or under section 167(6) or 174(6) of their decision not to make an assessment.**
>
> **(Regulation 11(1) and (2))**

> **Where under section 172(2) or 173(1) a parent asks the LEA to arrange for an assessment to be made under section 167, the LEA shall within six weeks of receiving that request give notice to the child's parent under section 167(4) of their decision to make an assessment, or under section 172(3)(a) or 173(2)(a) of their decision not to make an assessment and of the parent's right to appeal to the Tribunal against that decision.**
>
> **(Regulation 11(3))**

Consideration against the criteria

3:95. Drawing on the criteria set out above, the LEA must now decide whether the evidence from the child's parents and school suggests that a statutory assessment is required.

Decision not to make a statutory assessment

> **If the LEA decide not to assess the educational needs of the child concerned, they must give notice in writing to the child's parents of that decision.**
>
> **(Section 167(6))**

3:96. The decision not to make a statutory assessment may be a severe disappointment to the child's parents and may also be unwelcome to the child's school. The LEA should therefore write to the school, as well as the child's parents, giving full reasons for their decision. Parents who have formally requested a statutory assessment under section 172 or 173 may appeal to the SEN Tribunal against a decision not to make such an assessment. The LEA should endeavour to ensure that the parents fully understand the school-based stages and their monitoring and review arrangements. The LEA should offer any guidelines or suggest any action they consider would help the school to meet the child's needs. If it is clear that there is disagreement between the parents and the school about the child's progress and attainments at school, or about the need for statutory assessment, the LEA may wish to arrange a meeting between the parents and the school.

Decision to proceed with a statutory assessment

> **Where the LEA decide to proceed with a statutory assessment they must inform the parents of their decision and their reasons for it.**
>
> **(Section 167(4))**

3:97. At this point parents should be informed that as part of the process of putting together all the relevant advice, their child may be called for assessment. Parental agreement to a medical examination and psychological assessment should have already been sought (see 3:14). Parents should be informed of their right to be present with their child at any interview, test, medical or other assessment which is being conducted for the purpose of producing that advice and should be told of the time and place of appointments. Parents should be told that, whilst it is their right to be present, in certain circumstances it may be counterproductive: for instance, where a classroom observation is carried out as part of the assessment, a child will behave differently if his or her parent is present, which would negate the purpose of the observation.

Requests for advice

> **For the purpose of making a statutory assessment, the LEA shall seek written:**
>
> 1. **Parental advice**
>
> 2. **Educational advice**
>
> 3. **Medical advice**
>
> 4. **Psychological advice**
>
> 5. **Social services advice**
>
> 6. **Any other advice, such as the views of the child, which the LEA or any other body from whom advice is sought, consider desirable. In particular advice from the Service Children's Education Authority (SCEA) (see Glossary) is to be sought where the child's parent is a serving member of the armed forces.**
>
> **(Regulation 6)**

> **District health authorities and social services departments, when requested by the LEA to provide advice for the purpose of making a statutory assessment, must provide that advice within six weeks of the date of the request, except in prescribed circumstances.**
>
> **(Section 166(4) and Regulation 11(6))**

3:98. The LEA will now proceed to seek parental, educational, medical, psychological and social services advice. The LEA must always give to those from whom advice is sought copies of any representations made by or evidence provided by the child's parents under section 167(1)(d). The advice must not be influenced by consideration of the name of the school at which the child might eventually be placed. Placement will be determined by the LEA at a later stage and in the light of any preference stated by or representations made by the parents. But discussions between advisers and parents about the child's needs and the advisers' written advice may include consideration of various options, including the scope for mainstream education for the child and the type of school in which the child's needs might best be met, for example mainstream, special or residential. But such discussions and advice should not commit the LEA, nor preempt the parents' statement of a preference, any representations they might make or the LEA's eventual decision.

3:99. The LEA should also ascertain as far as possible what views the child has of his or her special needs and how these might best be addressed. **All requests for advice should be accompanied by notification of the date by which the advice must be submitted.**

Parental advice

3:100. Parents must be asked to give any advice they consider to be relevant. Parents may welcome guidance on how to contribute effectively to their child's assessment. The following guidelines, already used successfully by many parents, may be helpful, although some adjustment may be necessary according to the age of the child concerned, especially if under five:

Guidelines for parents' contributions to their child's statutory assessment

Introduction

These guidelines are to help you with your contribution to the assessment. You do not have to use them if you do not want to. You may change the order, leave bits out or add things you may feel to be important. We should find it helpful, however, if you used the headings we have suggested. Your written contribution may be as short or as long as you wish.

A – THE EARLY YEARS

1. What do you remember about the early years that might help?

2. What was he or she like as a young baby?

3. Were you happy about progress at the time?

4. When did you first feel things were not right?

5. What happened?

6. What advice or help did you receive – from whom?

B – WHAT IS YOUR CHILD LIKE NOW

1. **General Health** – Eating and sleeping habits; general fitness, absences from school, minor ailments – coughs and colds. Serious illnesses/accidents – periods in hospital. Any medicine or special diet? General alertness – tiredness, signs of use of drugs – smoking, drinking, glue-sniffing.

2. **Physical Skills** – Walking, running, climbing – riding a bike, football or other games, drawing pictures, writing, doing jigsaws; using construction kits, household gadgets, tools, sewing.

3. **Self-Help** – Level of personal independence – dressing, etc; making bed, washing clothes, keeping room tidy, coping with day-to-day routine; budgeting pocket money, general independence – getting out and about.

4. **Communication** – Level of speech, explains, describes events, people, conveys information (eg messages to and from school), joins in conversations; uses telephone.

5. **Playing and Learning at Home** – How ..... spends time, watching TV, reading for pleasure and information, hobbies, concentration, sharing.

6. **Activities Outside** – Belonging to clubs, sporting activities, happy to go alone.

7. **Relationships** – With parents, brothers and sisters; with friends; with other adults (friends and relations) at home generally, 'outside' generally.

   Is .... a loner?

8. **Behaviour at Home** – Co-operates, shares, listens to and and carries out requests, helps in the house, offers help, fits in with family routine and 'rules'. Moods good and bad, sulking – temper tantrums; demonstrative, affectionate.

9. **At School** – Relationships with other children and teachers; progress with reading, writing, number, other subjects and activities at school. How the school has helped/not helped with your child. Have you been asked to help with school work – hearing child read – with what result?

   Does .... enjoy school?

   What does .... find easy or difficult?

C – YOUR GENERAL VIEWS

1. What do you think your child's special educational needs are?

2. How do you think these can be best provided for?

3. How do you compare your child with others of the same age?

4. What is your child good at or what does he or she enjoy doing?

5. What does .... worry about – is .... aware of difficulties?

6. What are your worries, concerns?

7. Is there any other information you would like to give

   a) About the family – major events that might have affected your child?

   b) Reports from other people?

8. With whom would you like more contact?

9. How do you think your child's needs affect the needs of the family as a whole?

3:101. Parents may find it helpful to talk to the Named LEA Officer whom the LEA nominated when the proposal to assess the child was first made. The role of the Named LEA Officer will be particularly important if the parents have difficulty in writing; if their first language is not English or Welsh; or if they have difficulty in preparing a written report. Following discussions with the parents, the Named LEA Officer should prepare a note of their views, which should be agreed by the parents before it is included in advice relating to the assessment.

3:102. If parents are advised and supported from the start, there should be fewer anxieties and disagreements about the proposed statement, if issued, and a stronger bond of agreement about the best way forward for the child. To that end, when a Named Person has been identified at an early stage, LEAs should encourage parents to seek the help of their Named Person in preparing their advice and should welcome the Named Person at any meetings. LEAs should also work closely with local parent or other voluntary organisations in order to develop partnership and support systems and information material on which parents may draw when assessments and statements are being made.

Educational advice

3:103. Advice must be sought from the school which the child is currently attending, any other school attended in the preceding 18 months and if appropriate, from those responsible for providing education otherwise than at school, for example, the LEA's home tuition service. The LEA must ask the school(s) to provide relevant information about the child and evidence of the school's identification and assessment of and provision for the child's special educational needs.

3:104. If schools follow the guidance set out in Part 2, they will be able to react quickly and effectively to an LEA's request for advice and will have to hand much of the necessary advice which the LEA will seek. A summary of the records of the school's work with a child at each stage should be appended to the educational advice.

3:105. In the light of the evidence received from the school, the LEA should consider whether they should seek separate advice from a teacher or professional from a learning support service involved with the child over the past year. This should usually be the specialist working with the child and the school at the stage before referral for statutory assessment. If it appears to the LEA that the child is visually and/or hearing impaired, the LEA must obtain educational advice from a teacher qualified to teach classes of visually and/or hearing impaired children.

Medical advice

3:106. In all cases the LEA must seek advice on all aspects of a child's health and development from the health service. In practice, the LEA will normally approach the designated medical officer for special educational needs (see paragraph 2:42). This doctor should coordinate the advice from all the health professionals concerned. Medical advice may include advice from the child's general practitioner and the school doctor and from therapists, school nurses, health visitors, other community nurses, child and adolescent mental health workers, and all other medical specialists who might be involved, for example orthopaedic surgeons and paediatric neurologists. Parents may also submit reports made by private professionals if they wish. The LEA must consider these reports in parallel with the professional advice provided by the designated medical officer.

3:107. The contribution of the health services to assessment is crucial. Medical advice may include information on:

i.   a medical condition which is likely to affect future learning ability

ii. medical treatment which is likely to affect the child's future learning ability

iii. general health or developmental problems which may relate to social conditions (for example social and family disadvantage)

iv. mental health problems which may cause emotional and behavioural difficulties

v.   shorter term but acute medical problems (for example, treatment for childhood cancer or recovery from serious trauma) which may necessitate special arrangements being made for a child, but with the understanding that the child's special needs are likely to be temporary and that the child will resume full participation in school within a reasonable period of time.

3:108. Any medical advice should state the likely consequences for the child's education and may include:

i.   information on any aspects of the child's medical condition which may affect his or her progress in school and advice on how best to manage the condition in the school context (for example the management of epilepsy or of a tracheotomy)

ii. advice on any special aid or equipment which the child may need

iii. information on the child's welfare and safety such as advice on the management of incontinence; feeding; independence and risk taking; and participation and supervision in the playground, while swimming and bathing, and taking part in out-of-school activities, and

iv. advice on any non-educational provision which may be needed.

3:109. Where a child has a serious or life-threatening condition such as muscular dystrophy or cystic fibrosis, medical advice should be sought about his or her condition. Care should be taken to ensure that parents are sensitively informed of the probable outcomes. It is not satisfactory for parents first to receive the information about their child's condition (with possible reference to terminal illness) when they see the draft statement.

3:110. Community nurses and health visitors have much to contribute in supporting parents during and after assessment. School nurses can provide practical advice to teachers and parents on the management of a particular child. GPs are becoming increasingly involved in child health surveillance for children up to age five and GP fund holders will sometimes be responsible for contracting for community nursing and therapeutic services. Many children additionally will attend child development centres or teams on a regular basis. The designated medical officer for special educational needs will be responsible for coordinating the contributions of all health care professionals and ensuring that they have access to up-to-date information on the full range of services provided by the LEA in order to inform and reassure parents about the assessment process. Consent should be obtained to the disclosure of medical information as in paragraph 2:52.

3:111. For some children with complex needs or specific disabilities or medical conditions, a health perspective will be crucial both in the initial assessment and in any subsequent reviews. The health services should:

i.   ensure that there are no additional difficulties or disabilities affecting the child, and monitor the child's general health and development

ii. help parents and teachers to understand the child's disability or medical condition and provide counselling and support to parents and children if required

iii. provide access to any specialist advice or services as required, and

iv. advise on any other matters such as access; provision of equipment; and administration of medication.

3:112. In these circumstances, the health services will not only contribute relevant information on the child's special needs, but may also contribute to the setting of objectives and the review process.

Psychological advice

3:113. The views of an educational psychologist are essential in fully assessing a child's special educational needs and in planning for any future provision. The educational psychologist from whom the advice is sought must be employed or engaged for the purpose by the LEA. In making his or her report, the educational psychologist should address a wide range of factors which may affect a child's functioning. Such factors may include the child's cognitive functioning; communication skills; perceptual skills; adaptive and personal and social skills; the child's approaches and attitudes to learning; his or her educational attainments; and the child's self-image, interests and behaviour. Educational psychologists may need to liaise with occupational therapists and physiotherapists for advice when investigating motor skills and their relationship to perceptual skills.

3:114. In some instances, the educational psychology service will have had a long-term relationship with a particular child and will be able to contribute a considerable body of opinion about the child's progress. In other cases, in addition to examining the child, it may be necessary for the educational psychologist to observe the child over a period of time in order to formulate a clear picture of his or her needs. As part of these observations and depending on the age of the child, the educational psychologist may wish to visit the child and parents at home.

3:115. The educational psychologist from whom the LEA seeks advice must consult, and record any advice received from, any other psychologist, such as a clinical or occupational psychologist, who he or she believes to have relevant knowledge of or information about the child. The LEA must consider any advice from a fully qualified educational psychologist commissioned independently and submitted by the parents.

Social services advice

3:116. The LEA will have copied the notice of their proposal to make a statutory assessment to the social services department. They must now seek advice as to whether the SSD is aware of any problems affecting the child or can provide advice and information on the child relevant to the assessment. The LEA should give social services departments full information on the LEA's statutory assessment arrangements and procedures. LEAs and social services departments should agree the procedures to be followed when the LEA notify a social services department of their proposal to assess a child's special educational needs.

3:117. Having been notified that the LEA will assess the child, the social services department should give the LEA any relevant information which they have about the family or the child.

In particular:

i.　if the SSD do not know the child and the family, and if they have no reason to suppose from evidence provided by the school or the LEA that they should seek further information, they should say so and need provide no further written advice. But social services departments may combine assessment of children 'in need' under Schedule 17 of the Children Act with statutory assessment under the 1993 Act. Therefore, given their general responsibilities for children 'in need' and their families and their duty to keep a register of children with disabilities, the social services department may wish to arrange a meeting with the child and his or her family to check whether:

　－　there are services they should provide for the child or family

　－　the family consider that the child should be registered as disabled (registration being wholly voluntary) and

　－　there is any further information the family should be given.

The results of any such meeting should be passed to the LEA as part of the social services department's advice for the statutory assessment

ii.　if the child is receiving social services provision such as day care or is living in a residential or foster home, the SSD should make available to the LEA any relevant observations, information and reports arising from such placements

iii.　if the child is 'looked after' by a local authority and therefore has a child care plan, the SSD should give the LEA full details of that care plan

iv.　if the child is in the care of a local authority and the local authority has parental responsibility, the SSD should ensure that any relevant information is provided and that social services staff attend assessments and medical examinations as appropriate

v.　if the child is, or may become, subject to child protection procedures, the SSD should give appropriate advice.

3:118. Social services departments should give LEAs information on services generally available for families of children 'in need' (as required under Schedule 1 of the Children Act) and should make available to the LEA any relevant information on planning processes or data collection (such as the register of Children with Disabilities or the Community Care Plan).

3:119. Even if the child is not currently known to social services, the LEA should inform the designated officer of the social services department if it seems likely that the child should be educated at a residential school. The social services department will wish to ensure that a parental request for residential education is not made on the basis of lack of support and practical help in their local community and that proper arrangements are made to ensure family contact if the child is placed outside the authority in question.

Involvement of the child

3:120. The LEA will wish to establish the views of children and young people themselves on their special educational needs and the way in which they might be met. The LEA may consider providing a pupil report form for the purpose. Pupils who are able to do so could submit their views themselves on such a form. Others may need the help of a parent, teacher, educational psychologist, social worker or other confidant, such as the Named Person. In other cases the adults closest to the child have a responsibility to establish to the best of their ability the wishes and feelings of the child, for example by interpreting the child's behaviour in different settings as a measure of the child's preferences. However they are ascertained, the wishes and feelings of the child have a separate identity and, even though they may overlap or coincide with the views of others, the LEA may wish to have the child's views set out separately from those of the parents and professionals.

Any other advice

3:121. The LEA should follow up the parents' suggestions of other agencies or individuals who might be called upon for advice (see 3:11). In addition, the LEA should approach any other body whom they consider could helpfully contribute to the accurate and timely assessment of the child in question. In particular, advice from the Service Children's Education Authority (SCEA) must be sought where the child's parent is a serving member of the armed forces.

4. Statement of Special Education Needs

Where, in the light of a section 167 assessment, it is necessary for the LEA to determine the special educational provision which the child's learning difficulty calls for, the LEA shall make and maintain a statement of his or her special educational needs.

(Section 168(1))

Criteria for Deciding to Draw up a Statement

4:1. Part 3 has dealt with the conduct of statutory assessment and the gathering of advice from agencies and individuals. Following the receipt of all the advice, the LEA must decide whether to draw up a statement. In a small number of cases, the LEA may decide that the degree of the child's learning difficulty or disability, and the nature of the provision necessary to meet the child's special educational needs, require the LEA to determine the child's special educational provision through making a statement.

4:2. The main ground on which an LEA may decide that they must make a statement is when the LEA conclude that all the special educational provision necessary to meet the child's needs cannot reasonably be provided within the resources normally available to mainstream schools in the area.

4:3. Most mainstream schools should have within their delegated budget some funding which reflects the additional needs of pupils with special educational needs. LEA-maintained schools should receive this through local management schemes which are weighted for the incidence of special educational needs within the authority. Grant-maintained schools receive this through their Annual Maintenance Grant (AMG), whether through LMS replication or from the Common Funding Formula.

4:4. In many instances, the issuing of a statement will entail the LEA making additional resources available to a mainstream school. But some LEA-maintained schools have delegated funds to meet the needs of pupils with statements, as have some GM schools where their AMG is determined by replication of the LEA's local management scheme. Clearly, the delegation to schools of funds for pupils with statements should not preclude the making of statements on the grounds that such funds are already within schools' budgets. But the making of a statement in such cases may not entail the LEA making additional resources available to those schools, except insofar as the LEA will be responsible for monitoring the child's progress and reviewing the statement, and thereby maintaining a continuing oversight of the child. Even where funding for pupils with statements is not delegated to schools, there may occasionally be instances when the LEA may conclude that it is necessary to make a statement in order to bring to bear the LEA's capacity to monitor the progress of a child through multidisciplinary involvement in the annual review process and other means.

4:5. Regardless of whether funding for pupils with statements is delegated to schools, responsibility for arranging the necessary provision rests with the LEA. When funding is delegated, LMS schemes must include conditions requiring governing bodies to ensure that *all* the provision specified in the statement is made. Schemes should also set out the necessary arrangements whereby the LEA will satisfy themselves that these conditions are being met.

4:6. As with the criteria for proceeding to a statutory assessment, the guidance set out below provides a framework within which it is important that schools, LEAs and other agencies involved develop the detail of local interpretation. Some LEAs have already reached agreements with schools about the level of resources that a school may be expected to expend on provision to meet the ascertained special educational needs of its pupils. In some LEAs this has been expressed as a percentage of the value of the pupil-led element of the school's annual budget. LEAs and schools may wish to develop measures of this type that will support decision-making at a local level about the precise level of resources that may be expected to be provided from within schools' budgets.

4:7. To help ensure consistency in the administration of criteria for statutory assessment at a local level, the Code suggests that LEAs consider setting up moderating groups – see paragraph 3:48. Such groups should be broadly representative of head teachers, should include representation from health and social services and may include others such as SEN coordinators, teachers, governors and educational psychologists. LEAs may wish to extend the remit of such groups to encourage consistent decisions about whether to make statements. Groups would not make decisions in individual cases, but, through sampling and retrospective comparison, would help make LEA practice more robust and clearly understood by schools and parents.

4:8. In deciding whether to draw up a statement the LEA should consider all the information emerging from the statutory assessment in the light of the evidence put forward by the school at the beginning of the assessment.

4:9. LEAs may therefore wish to ask the following questions:

i. **the child's learning difficulties**

   – is the information on the child's learning difficulties that emerges from the statutory assessment broadly in accord with the evidence presented by the school for consideration by the LEA?

   – if not, are there aspects of the child's learning difficulties which the school may have overlooked and which, with the benefit of advice, equipment or other provision, the school could effectively address within its own resources?

ii. **the child's special educational provision**

   – do the proposals for the child's special educational provision emerging from the statutory assessment indicate that the special educational provision being made by the school, including teaching strategies or other approaches, is appropriate to the child's learning difficulties?

   – if not, are there approaches which, with the benefit of advice, equipment or other provision, the school could effectively adopt within its own resources?

Consideration of the provision that may need to be made

4:10. If the statutory assessment confirms that the assessment and provision made by the school are appropriate, but the child is nonetheless not progressing, or not progressing sufficiently well, the LEA should consider what further provision may be needed and whether that provision can be made within the school's resources.

4:11. The following exemplars may help the LEA in deciding whether a statement is necessary:

i. if, as a result of a statutory assessment, the LEA conclude that, for example, the child's learning difficulties call for:

   – occasional advice to the school from an external specialist

   – occasional support with personal care from a non-teaching assistant

   – access to a particular piece of equipment such as a portable word-processing device, an electronic keyboard or a tape-recorder, or

   – minor building alterations such as widening a doorway or improving the acoustic environment

   the LEA may conclude that the school could reasonably be expected to make such provision from within its own resources

ii. but if, as a result of a statutory assessment, the LEA conclude that, for example, the child requires:

   – regular direct teaching by a specialist teacher

   – daily individual support from a non-teaching assistant

   – a significant piece of equipment such as a closed circuit television or a computer or CD-ROM device with appropriate ancillaries and software

   – a major building adaptation such as the installation of a lift, or

   – the regular involvement of non-educational agencies

   the LEA may conclude that the school could **not** reasonably be expected to make such provision within its own resources and that the nature of the provision suggests that the LEA should formally identify in a statement the child's needs, the full range of provision to be made and the review arrangements that will apply. The LEA's conclusions will, of course, depend on the precise circumstances of each case, taking into account arrangements for funding schools in the area

iii. if, as a result of a statutory assessment, the LEA conclude that a change of placement may be indicated for the child, even if such a change involves moving from a mainstream school to a specialist unit at the same school or from one mainstream school to another, then the LEA should consider drawing up a statement

iv. if, as a result of a statutory assessment of a child of parents in the armed forces, the LEA conclude that the parents' frequent moves might significantly disrupt effective special educational provision for the child, the LEA should consider drawing up a statement

v.   if, as a result of a statutory assessment, the LEA conclude that a day or residential special school placement might be necessary, the LEA should draw up a statement.

4:12.   The decision as to whether to make a statement should be determined by the child's identifiable special educational needs in the context of arrangements for funding schools in the area. LEAs should, of course, arrange for the provision specified in a child's statement to be made in a cost-effective manner, but that provision must be consistent with the child's assessed needs. The efficient use of resources must be taken into account when an LEA is considering the placement of a child with a statement, once the parents have had an opportunity to express a preference – see paragraphs 4:40 – 4:59.

Assessment and emergency placements

4:13.   Where a child arriving unexpectedly in the LEA exhibits such significant learning difficulties as would normally warrant a statement, the LEA should consult the parents and those immediately concerned, including the previous LEA, about the most appropriate placement. The LEA should place the child where they consider the child's needs may most appropriately be met. At the same time the LEA should initiate a statutory assessment. On completion of the assessment, the LEA should consider whether a statement is necessary as well as the suitability of the placement. If the child has been placed and will remain in a special school, a statement should always be made.

4:14.   In exceptional cases it may be necessary to make an emergency placement for a child, for example where:

a.   the child's medical circumstances have changed suddenly, causing a rapid and serious deterioration in the child's health or development

b.   the parents, school, relevant professionals and the LEA agree that a sudden and serious deterioration in the child's behaviour make the child's current placement untenable or unsafe.

4:15.   An emergency placement should be made only when the LEA, parents, school and any relevant professionals who will be involved in the statutory assessment are all agreed that the child's needs are such that action must be taken immediately and an emergency placement is the best way forward.

4:16.   When an emergency placement is made, the LEA should immediately initiate a statutory assessment. It is likely that the assessment will conclude that a statement should be made. If, however, the assessment concludes that a statement is not necessary, the child's emergency placement should be reconsidered. Decisions about how the child's needs should be best met in the longer term should not be prejudiced by the nature of the emergency placement. Statements drawn up in these circumstances should include detailed objectives with clearly specified review arrangements to monitor the efficacy of the provision made for the child. Whilst the LEA have a duty to review the statement on an annual basis, they may wish to use their powers to review more frequently and to ask for interim reports on the child's progress.

Decision not to issue a statement: the note in lieu

> **Where an LEA, having carried out an assessment of a child, decide not to make a statement, they shall within two weeks of the date on which the assessment was completed, write to the child's parents with their decision and tell the parents of their right to appeal to the Tribunal against the decision.**
>
> **(Section 169(1) and Regulation 14(1))**

4:17. The statutory assessment process may lead the LEA to the conclusion that the child's special educational needs can be met from within the school's own resources, with or without the intervention of a professional service from outside the school. The decision not to issue a statement may be disappointing to parents and seen as a denial of additional resources for their child. Parents may appeal to the Tribunal over a decision not to issue a statement. The LEA should ensure that parents are aware that resources are available within all maintained schools to meet the majority of special needs of their pupils and that parents fully understand the school-based stages of assessment and the monitoring and review arrangements which will ensure that their child's needs are met by the school, with external support if necessary, in an appropriate way.

4:18. The statutory assessment will have contributed significantly to the school's, parents' and the LEA's knowledge of the child. The LEA should therefore consider issuing **a note in lieu of a statement**.

4:19. In such a note the LEA should set out the reasons for their conclusions, with supporting evidence from the statutory assessment of the child. All advice collected as part of the statutory assessment should be sent to the parents, and, subject to their agreement, to the child's school and any other professionals who have given advice during the assessment process. This procedure will put to good use the information that emerges from the child's statutory assessment. The information can be used by those working with the child in school to augment their strategies for meeting the child's special educational needs. The LEA may wish to arrange a meeting with the parents and the school to discuss the decision and the note.

4:20. In some cases, the LEA may be able to decide very quickly that it is not necessary to make a statement: parents should be informed – by the issue of a written notice under section 169(1) – immediately. The LEA should always give their reasons. But the writing of a comprehensive and useful note in lieu will very often require quite as much thought and time as the drafting of a proposed statement. Indeed, the conclusion as to whether to make a statement or issue a note in lieu may become clear only when the LEA officer marshals all the information and sets out in writing the child's educational and non-educational needs and the provision required to meet those needs.

4:21. There may therefore be advantage in the format of the note in lieu broadly following the statutory format of the statement, although it will always be essential to make clear the different legal status of the two documents.

4:22. Thus, while the layout of a note in lieu is a matter for the LEA concerned, the first part of such a note might describe the child's special educational needs, with supporting evidence attached in the form of the parental, educational, medical and psychological advice, any advice from the social services department and any other advice gathered during the assessment, such as the views of the child. The second part of the note might set out the LEA's reasons for declining to make a statement and offer guidance as to the special educational provision which might appropriately be made for the child, with specialist advice if necessary, but without being determined by the LEA. The third part might then, again reflecting the advice received and appended, and agreement between the LEA and the agencies concerned, describe any non-educational needs and appropriate provision.

4:23. The statutory assessment process ends when the LEA decide whether they will make a statement. That decision must normally be taken within ten weeks of the issue of a notice under section 167(4). The statutory time limits within which the LEA must either inform parents that they will not make a statement or issue to parents a proposed statement are then the same: normally, no more than two weeks after making their decision and no more than 12 weeks after the issue of a notice under section 167(4) that they will make a statutory assessment, the LEA must either:

i. issue a notice under section 169(1) that they will not make a statement, or

ii. issue a proposed statement, together with a written notice under Schedule 10, paragraph 2.

Writing the Statement

> **Where an LEA, having made an assessment of a child, decide to make a statement, they shall serve a copy of a proposed statement and a written notice on the child's parent under paragraph 2 of Schedule 10 within two weeks of the date on which the assessment was completed.**
>
> **(Regulation 14(1))**

4:24. The notice must be in the form prescribed in Part A of the Schedule to the Regulations. The statement of special educational needs must follow the format and contain the information prescribed by the Regulations.

Part 1   *Introduction* The child's name and address and date of birth. The child's home language and religion. The names and address(es) of the child's parents.

Part 2   *Special Educational Needs* (learning difficulties). Details of each and every one of the child's special educational needs as identified by the LEA during statutory assessment and on the advice received and attached as appendices to the statement.

Part 3   *Special Educational Provision* The special educational provision which the LEA consider necessary to meet the child's special educational needs.

     a)   The *objectives* which the special educational provision should aim to meet.

     b)   The *special educational provision* which the LEA consider appropriate to meet the needs specified in Part 2 and to meet the specified objectives.

     c)   The arrangements to be made for monitoring progress in meeting those objectives, particularly for setting short-term targets for the child's progress and for reviewing his or her progress on a regular basis.

Part 4   *Placement* The type and name of school where the special educational provision specified in Part 3 is to be made or the arrangements for the education to be made otherwise than in school.

Part 5   *Non-Educational Needs* All relevant non-educational needs of the child as agreed between the health services, social services or other agencies and the LEA.

Part 6   *Non-Educational Provision* Specification of relevant non-educational provision required to meet the non-educational needs of the child as agreed between the health services and/or social services and the LEA, including the agreed arrangements for its provision.

     Signature and date

     APPENDICES

(Regulation 13 and Part B of the Schedule to the Regulations)

4:25. All the advice obtained and taken into consideration during the assessment process must be attached as appendices to the statement:

The advice appended to the statement must include:

1. **Parental representations, evidence and advice**

2. **Educational advice**

3. **Medical advice**

4. **Psychological advice**

5. **Social services advice**

6. **Any other advice, such as the views of the child, which the LEA or any other body from whom advice is sought consider desirable. In particular, where the child's parent is a serving member of the armed forces, advice from the Service Children's Education Authority (SCEA).**

(Regulation 13)

4:26. LEAs should draft clear, unambiguous statements. Where diagnostic or technical terms are necessary or helpful, for example in referring to specific disabilities, their meaning should be amplified in terms which parents and other non-professionals will readily understand. LEAs should take particular care to ensure that the text is placed in the correct part, so as to correspond with the form set out in Part B of the Schedule to the Education (Special Educational Needs) Regulations 1994.

Part 2: Special educational needs (learning difficulties)

4:27. Part 2 of the statement should describe all the child's learning difficulties identified during the statutory assessment. It should also include a description of the child's functioning – what the child can and cannot do. The description in Part 2 should draw on and may refer to the professional advice attached in the appendices. Where the LEA adopt that advice in their description of the child's learning difficulties, they should say that they have done so but merely stating that they are adopting the advice in the appendices is not sufficient. The appendices may contain conflicting opinion or opinion open to interpretation, which the LEA must resolve, giving reasons for the conclusions they have reached.

Part 3: Special educational provision

4:28. Part 3 of the statement is divided into three sub-sections:

- in the **first sub-section**, the LEA should set out the main educational and developmental objectives to be achieved by the special educational provision over the expected duration of the statement

- the **second sub-section** should set out *all* the special educational provision that the LEA consider appropriate for *all* the learning difficulties identified in Part 2, even where some of the provision is to be made by direct intervention on the part of the authority and some is to be made by the child's school within its own resources. It may be helpful for the LEA to specify which elements of the provision are to be made by the school, and which elements are to be made by the LEA. The LEA will be responsible for arranging all the special educational provision specified in the statement

This sub-section should also specify in accordance with section 18 of the Education Reform Act 1988 any modifications or disapplications of the provisions of the National Curriculum (in terms of attainment targets, programmes of study and assessment arrangements) which the LEA consider necessary to meet the child's special educational needs, with details as to how a broad and balanced curriculum is to be maintained. From September 1995 it will no longer be necessary for statements to modify National Curriculum provisions to enable a child to study at a lower level on the 10-point scale than applies to most of the pupils working within the same key stage

For pupils whose assessment is close to their preparation date for GCSEs or vocational examinations, this sub-section should also indicate any special examination provision recommended to enable the pupil to have full access to the examination and properly demonstrate his or her attainment, and for which special approval will have to be sought from the Examining Group in advance of the examination. It should be noted, however, that a pupil does not require a statement in order to benefit from any concessions that an Examination Group might grant to a pupil with special educational needs

The provision set out in this sub-section should normally be specific, detailed and quantified (in terms, for example, of hours of ancillary or specialist teaching support) although there will be cases where some flexibility should be retained in order to meet the changing special educational needs of the child concerned

— the **third sub-section** should specify the arrangements to be made for setting short-term educational targets. The targets themselves should not be part of the statement. By their nature, the targets will require regular revision, while the longer term objectives in the first sub-section remain stable. Targets should be set by the child's school, in consultation with his or her parents, within two months of the child's placement. The child's achievements in the light of those targets should then be considered at the first annual review and new targets set

This sub-section should also specify any special arrangements for the annual review and recognise the need for the monitoring and evaluation of the child's progress during the course of the year.

4:29. It is important that all the information in Part 3 should be easily understood by all involved in the child's education, including the parents.

Part 4: Placement

4:30. In the final statement Part 4 will specify the type of school and any particular school which the LEA consider appropriate for the child, or the provision for education otherwise than at school which the LEA consider appropriate. But this Part must be left blank when the proposed statement is issued, so that the LEA do not preempt their consideration of any preference for a maintained school which the parents may state or any representation the parents may make in favour of a non-maintained special school (see Glossary) or an independent school.

Part 5: Non-educational needs

4:31. Part 5 should specify any non-educational needs of the child which the LEA either propose to meet or are satisfied will be met, by arrangement or otherwise, by the health services, social services department or some other body.

Part 6: Non-educational provision

4:32. Part 6 should specify the non-educational provision which is required to meet the needs identified in Part 5 and which the LEA either propose to make available or are satisfied will be purchased by the district health authority, GP fund holders or others. The designated medical officer for special educational needs should liaise as necessary to ensure that the health service contribution has been confirmed. Part 6 should also state the objectives to be achieved by such non-educational provision and should set out the arrangements which have been agreed by the LEA and the providing body for its delivery.

4:33. When considering a child's non-educational needs and provision, the LEA should ensure that the needs are clearly and accurately described and that there is full agreement on the nature and quantity of the provision necessary to meet those needs, consulting the relevant responsible professionals as necessary.

Speech and language therapy

4:34. Speech and language therapy may be regarded as either educational or non-educational provision, depending upon the health or developmental history of each child. Prime responsibility for the provision of speech and language therapy services to children rests with the NHS. This applies generally and also to any specification of such services in a statement of special educational needs, whether in Part 3 as educational provision or in Part 6 as non-educational provision. District health authorities and GP fund holders are responsible for purchasing therapy services through the contracts they make with providers of health care (NHS Trusts). The NHS provides a professionally-managed speech and language therapy service, covering pre-school, school-age and adult age groups and which has close links with the other child health services.

4:35. Where the NHS does not provide speech and language therapy for a child whose statement specifies such therapy as educational provision, ultimate responsibility for ensuring that the provision is made rests with the LEA, unless the child's parents have made appropriate alternative arrangements. Schools, LEAs and the NHS should cooperate closely in meeting the needs of children with communication difficulties.

4:36. It is important that the nature and extent of provision required for individual children should be examined very carefully and that full consideration is given as to how such provision can best be delivered. In some cases, for example, children may need regular and continuing help from a speech therapist, either individually or in a group. In other cases, it may be appropriate for staff at the child's school to deliver a programme of support under the guidance and supervision of a speech therapist.

The proposed statement

> **Before making a statement, the LEA shall issue to the parents a copy of the proposed statement, and a notice setting out the arrangements for the choice of school, the parents' right to make representations about the content of the statement, and their right to appeal to the Tribunal against the contents of the final statement. In that notice, the LEA must include details of schools approved under section 189 of the Act and of non-maintained schools; and of maintained schools in the area which cater for children of the appropriate age.**
>
> **(Schedule 10 paragraph 2, Regulations 12 and 13)**

> **The period from the service of a proposed statement and written notice under schedule 10,2 to the service of a copy of a statement under schedule 10,6 shall be no more than eight weeks.**
>
> **(Regulation 14(2))**

4:37. The LEA must draw up a proposed statement, completing all Parts except Part 4: the proposed statement must not contain any details relating to where the proposed special educational provision should be made.

4:38. The LEA must send the proposed statement and copies of the advice which has been submitted during the assessment to the child's parents. At the same time, the LEA must send the parents a notice in the form prescribed in Part A of the Schedule to the regulations, which sets out the procedures to be followed, including procedures for naming the appropriate school. Copies of the proposed statement should also be sent to all those who have given advice during the making of the statement.

4:39. When making a statement, LEAs should remember the needs of parents and children whose first language is not English or Welsh. Where children have different linguistic and cultural backgrounds, LEAs should seek advice from bilingual support staff, and teachers of English as a second language, interpreters and translators and other local sources of advice as appropriate, to help ensure that such parents and children are involved in all aspects of the process. For example, the LEA should consider translating letters sent to parents, and the draft statements, into the parents' first language.

Naming a school

Parents may express a preference for the school in the maintained sector they wish their child to attend, or make representations for a placement outside the maintained sector. LEAs must comply with a parental preference unless the school is unsuitable to the child's age, ability, aptitude or special educational needs, or the placement would be incompatible with the efficient education of the other children with whom the child would be educated, or with the efficient use of resources. LEAs must consider parental representations and arrange any meeting(s) the parents seek, before issuing the final statement.

(Schedule 10, paras 3-5(1), Regulations 12 to 14)

4:40. The LEA must explain to parents the arrangements for expressing a preference for a particular school under paragraph 3 of Schedule 10 of the Act and the LEA's qualified duty to comply with that preference. Paragraph 4 of the same Schedule gives parents the right to make representations, which the LEA must consider, about the content of the statement; and the right to request meetings to discuss any aspect of the content of the proposed statement, including the advice obtained during the statutory assessment.

4:41. Three considerations govern the naming of a school in a statement: the placement must be appropriate to the child's needs, while also compatible with the interests of other children already in the school and with the efficient use of the LEA's resources.

4:42. Under section 160 of the Act, LEAs have a qualified duty to secure that children with special educational needs, including children with statements, are educated in mainstream schools. If parents express a preference for a mainstream school, the LEA must comply with that preference so long as the three conditions in paragraph 4:41 are met. If those conditions do not apply in the mainstream school preferred by the child's parents but would apply in another, the LEA must name that alternative school, in fulfilment of its duty under section 160. If, however, the conditions would not apply in any mainstream school, the LEA will look to a special school placement or alternative arrangements.

4:43. Parents may, of course, express a preference for a maintained special school. If they do so, the LEA no longer have a duty under section 160 to secure a mainstream education for the child. But neither do the parents have a veto on mainstream education: all will depend upon the three criteria in paragraph 4:41 above, considered in the light of a thorough assessment of the child's special educational needs and the provision necessary to meet them.

4:44. The LEA must comply with a parental preference for a maintained special school so long as the three conditions – appropriateness for the child and compatibility with the interests of other children and the efficient use of resources – are met. But if a special school would be unsuitable for the child, or his or her attendance at the special school would be unsuitable for other children there or would involve the inefficient use of the LEA's resources, the LEA are not obliged to comply with the parents' preference and may name either another special school or a mainstream school, whichever would better meet the three conditions.

4:45. The LEA should inform parents that all maintained schools must publish information on their policies on special educational needs. The LEA should encourage parents both to visit schools and to see the policies and any other relevant documentation to assist them in stating their preference. Discussions with other parents may be helpful. Parent/teacher associations, local voluntary organisations and parent partnership schemes may be able to offer additional information, practical advice and counselling if required. In some circumstances, and if parents request such help, an officer of the LEA may wish to visit particular schools with parents to ensure that their questions and concerns are dealt with effectively and promptly and to make certain that they fully understand the range of provision that the schools can offer.

4:46. When LEAs send parents a copy of the proposed statement, they must tell the parents that they have the right to make representations to the LEA in favour of a school outside the maintained sector and that, if they wish to make such representations, they should do so within 15 days of receiving the proposed statement. If the LEA do not agree to the parents' representations, they should inform the parents of their decision before naming any school in the final statement. Parents will then have the opportunity to express a preference for a maintained school under paragraph 3 of Schedule 10 if they wish to do so.

4:47. When LEAs send parents a copy of the proposed statement, they must also send parents a list of all LEA-maintained and grant-maintained schools within the area of the LEA which cater for children of the appropriate age. They may also send parents a list of all such schools in neighbouring areas. LEAs must inform parents of the names of all independent schools approved under section 189 of the Act and of all non-maintained special schools. The Department for Education and the Welsh Office Education Department will make comprehensive lists of such schools available to LEAs on a regular basis.

4:48. If the parents make representations in favour of a non-maintained special school or an independent school, an officer of the LEA should discuss with them why they believe that school should be named. If naming the school in question would provide the child with residential education, the LEA should discuss with the parents why they feel such provision is necessary to meet the child's special educational needs and, if appropriate, may choose to involve the social services department in discussing the child's wider needs with the family. If parents have not visited the school and wish to do so, an officer of the LEA should help arrange such a visit.

4:49. In some instances the parents may not have understood that a school within the LEA could provide a similar programme. Where parents are unsure about a choice of school or are unhappy about the choice of a school within the LEA, it may be particularly helpful to ensure that they can talk both to an officer of the LEA and to a parent adviser or counsellor from a local parent partnership scheme or from a voluntary organisation. Taking parents' concerns seriously may ensure that there is mutual understanding and respect and may help to avoid conflict. In some instances, parents may value a number of meetings to review the options and to talk through their concerns. Where the LEA hold more than one meeting with the parents to consider representations on the proposed statement, the eight week time limit within which the final statement must be issued will not apply. The LEA should, however, make every effort to arrange meetings quickly and issue the final statement promptly.

4:50. The LEA should consider very carefully a preference stated by parents for a denominational mainstream maintained school and representations made by parents for a denominational non-maintained special school or independent school. Denominational considerations cannot override the three criteria which the LEA must apply in deciding the school which should be named in the statement – appropriateness to the child's needs, compatibility with the efficient education of other children and compatibility with the efficient use of resources. But denominational considerations may influence the appropriateness of a school for meeting the child's needs and the child's ability to thrive in and benefit from a particular school. The LEA should take such considerations into account when two or more schools, one of which has a denominational affiliation favoured by the parents, could meet the three governing criteria.

4:51. It is important that the spiritual development of all children, including those with special educational needs, is addressed as part of their education. To help meet this requirement, every pupil attending either a mainstream or special school must receive religious education and attend religious worship, unless this would be against the wishes of the parents.

4:52. If it is agreed that a residential school should be named in the statement, the LEA and parent should also agree the arrangements for the child's contact with his or her family and for any special help, such as transport, which may be needed to maintain home/school contact. The question of residential placements is covered more fully in the Circular: 'The Education of Pupils with Emotional and Behavioural Difficulties'.

4:53. The LEA and the child's parents may conclude that the child should be placed in an independent school which is not approved by the Secretary of State under section 189. In such cases, the LEA must seek the Secretary of State's consent to such a placement and should do so before naming the school in the final copy of the statement. The Secretary of State aims to make a decision within two weeks of the date on which such a request for his consent was sent. Should the Secretary of State take more than two weeks, the LEA are not bound by the eight week time limit governing the issue of the final statement. Nor will the time limit apply if the Secretary of State declines to give his consent to a proposed placement and a request is made for the Secretary of State's consent to a placement at another independent school which is not approved under section 189.

4:54. Where the LEA decide that the final statement will not name the parents' first choice of school, the LEA should explain that decision in writing to the parents. Visits by parents to the school proposed by the LEA with an opportunity to discuss their child's special needs with the head teacher, SEN coordinator or any specialist teaching staff may be helpful. Parents' concerns and disappointments should be taken seriously, and every effort should be made to provide any additional information and advice or to arrange any further visits which will help them reach an informed decision about their child's future.

Consultation before naming a school in a statement

> **A local education authority shall, before specifying the name of any maintained, grant-maintained or grant-maintained special school in a statement, consult the governing body of the school, and if the school is maintained by another local education authority, that authority.**
>
> **(Schedule 10, Para 3(4))**

4:55. The LEA must consult a school before naming it in a statement. If the school is maintained by another authority, the LEA must also consult that authority. The LEA should give due consideration to the views expressed by those consulted, but the final decision as to whether to name the school falls to the LEA.

4:56. The LEA have a **duty** to name the parents' preferred school in a statement so long as the conditions set out in paragraph 4:41 apply: the placement must be appropriate to the child's age, ability, aptitude and special educational needs, while also compatible with the interests of other children already in the school and with the efficient use of the LEA's resources. But, for example, the LEA should **not** name a school in a statement if the school is selective, and the child does not meet the criteria for selection, because the placement would not be appropriate to the child's ability.

4:57. The governing body of the school can **not** refuse to admit a child solely because he or she has special educational needs.

4:58. The LEA should also consider carefully whether the admission of the child to a mainstream school would take the school over the number fixed as the number of intended admissions for the year, which must not be less than the 'standard number' or 'approved admissions number', in other words, whether the school is already nominally full. Admitting children over this number might be incompatible with the provision of efficient education or the efficient use of resources. The LEA should consider this point very carefully in cases where they are not the admissions authority for the school in question: that is, it is maintained by another authority, is voluntary aided or is grant maintained.

4:59. When the LEA decide not to name the parents' preferred school in a statement because the conditions in paragraph 4:41 do not apply, they should consult the parents about any other schools they would like their child to attend.

Transport costs for children with statements

4:60. The parents' preferred school may be further away from the child's home than another school which is appropriate to the child's special educational needs. In such a case it would be open to the LEA to name the nearer school, because that would be compatible with the efficient use of the LEA's resources. It would also be open to the LEA to name the school preferred by the child's parents, so long as the parents met the transport costs.

4:61. The school named in a child's statement must be capable of meeting the child's special educational needs. LEAs should not, therefore, promulgate general transport policies which seek to limit the schools for which parents of children with statements may express a preference if free transport is to be provided.

Education otherwise than at school

4:62. Section 163 of the Act empowers the LEA to arrange for some or all of a child's special educational provision to be made otherwise than at school. Section 164 enables the LEA to make arrangements for a child with a statement to attend an institution outside England and Wales: where they do so, the LEA may contribute to or pay the fees of the institution and the travelling and other expenses of the child and any person, including a parent, who might accompany the child.

4:63. The LEA should consider carefully any representations made by parents in favour of their child attending an establishment outside England and Wales. If the LEA consider that some or all of a child's special educational provision should be made otherwise than at school, or if they agree that the child should attend an institution outside England and Wales, they may specify those arrangements in Part 4 of the statement.

Children educated at parents' expense

4:64. Parents may choose to place a child with a statement in an independent school (whether or not approved under section 189) or a non-maintained special school at their own expense. If parents choose to make such provision for their child, the LEA must satisfy themselves that the school is able to make the special educational provision specified in the statement before they are relieved of their duty to arrange that provision. Once so satisfied, the LEA are under no obligation to contribute towards the cost of educating the child at the school of the parents' choice. The LEA are, however, still under a duty to maintain the child's statement and to review it annually, following the procedures set out in Part 6 below.

Parental representations over the proposed statement

4:65. If parents have been fully consulted at the earlier stages of assessment, they are more likely to consider that the proposed statement presents a positive and accurate appraisal of their child's special educational needs and that the provision proposed represents an appropriate response to those needs. The LEA should, however, inform parents that:

i. they may within 15 days make representations to the LEA, and require that a meeting be arranged with an officer of the LEA to discuss the contents of the statement

ii. within 15 days of meeting the officer, the parents may make further representations or, if they disagree with any part of the assessment, require further meetings to be arranged with appropriate people within the LEA to discuss the advice given

iii. within a final 15 days from the last meeting the parents can make further comments to the LEA.

4:66. Every effort should be made to ensure that parents are happy with the proposed statement and that they understand the background to the proposals made for their child and consider that their wishes and feelings have been given full and sensitive consideration. Similar effort should be made to ensure that, so far as possible, the child's views are reflected in the proposed statement and that the child understands the reasons for the proposals.

4:67. At any meetings arising from the proposed statement, LEA officers should give parents sufficient time and information in order to discuss their anxieties with the Named LEA Officer, and seek as far as possible to come to a mutual agreement. Some parents may find assessment very stressful and need additional personal support. LEAs should inform parents that they may be accompanied by friends or relatives, or their Named Person, at any meetings (see paragraph 3:11). The LEA may wish to refer parents to professionals in health or other services for clarification of any relevant aspect of the provision proposed which is giving cause for concern.

The final statement

> **Where an LEA make a statement, they shall serve a copy on the child's parents and give notice in writing of their right to appeal to the Tribunal against the description in the statement of the child's special educational needs, the special educational provision specified in the statement, and the school named or, if no school is named, that fact. The LEA must also give the parents the name of the person to whom they may apply for information and advice about the child's special educational needs.**
>
> **(Schedule 10, para 6)**

4:68. When amendments are suggested to the proposed statement and agreed by the LEA and the parents, the final statement should be issued immediately. LEAs must arrange the special educational provision, and may arrange any non-educational provision specified in the statement, from the date on which the statement is made. Every effort should be made to ensure that parents understand the significance of any amendments and the nature of the provision which is proposed to meet the child's special educational needs. Where, despite opportunities to discuss the situation with an officer of the LEA and any relevant professionals, the parents' proposals for amendments to the proposed statement are refused by the LEA, or the parents are unwilling to accept other amendments to the proposed statement, the LEA may nonetheless proceed to issue the final statement. The LEA must, however, inform the parents of their right to appeal to the Tribunal with regard to the provision specified in the statement, including the named school, and the procedures to be followed if they wish to do so.

4:69. Recourse to the Tribunal will inevitably be stressful for parents and time-consuming for the LEA concerned. To minimise appeals to the Tribunal, LEAs should ensure that parents have the fullest possible access to information and support during the statutory assessment process and that they are fully involved in contributing to their child's statement.

The Named Person

4:70. When the LEA send the parents the final version of the statement, they must inform the parents in writing of the name of the person who in future can give the parents advice and information about their child's special educational needs. This is the parents' **Named Person**.

4:71. Part 3 of this Code recommends that LEAs and parents might discuss the identity of the Named Person at the start of the assessment process. When parents so choose, the individual can then help them during the making of the assessment and any subsequent statement. Some parents may decide not to have a Named Person at this early stage; others may need the help of a voluntary organisation or parents' group in choosing their Named Person.

4:72. It is the LEA's responsibility to identify the Named Person when a statement is made. They should always seek to do so in cooperation with the parents. The Named Person should be someone whom the parents can trust. He or she should be capable of giving parents accurate information and sound advice. LEAs may wish to consult local voluntary organisations, parents' groups and relevant professionals in order to identify individuals who are willing to act as Named Persons.

4:73. If the parents decide that they do not wish to suggest a Named Person, the LEA must still give them the name of someone from whom advice and information can be obtained. There is no statutory restriction on the identity of the Named Person. Normally, however, there will be advantage in that person being someone who is independent of and who is not employed by the LEA. The role of the Named Person is not the same as that of the Named LEA Officer. Both help parents. But the Named Person acts as an independent adviser, while the Named LEA Officer acts as a source of information within the LEA. The Named Person might, therefore, be someone with whom the LEA works in a parent partnership scheme.

Keeping, disclosure and transfer of statements

A statement should not be disclosed without the consent of the child's parents except for certain statutory purposes or in the interests of the child.

(Regulation 19)

4:74. Statutory purposes include disclosure to the SEN Tribunal when parents appeal, and to the Secretary of State if parents make a complaint to him under the 1944 Act; disclosure on the order of any court or for the purpose of any criminal proceedings; disclosure for the purposes of investigations of maladministration under the Local Government Act 1974; disclosure to enable any authority to perform duties resulting from the Disabled Persons (Services, Consultation and Representation) Act 1986, or from the Children Act 1989 relating to safeguarding and promoting the welfare of children; and disclosure to OFSTED and OHMCI (Wales) inspection teams as part of their inspections of schools.

4:75. The interests of the child include the provision of information to the child's school and teachers. It is important that teachers working closely with the child should have a full knowledge of the child's statement; so too should the Careers Service officers who provide careers guidance to the child's school and who participate in reviews of the child's statement. LEAs may also give access to the statement to persons engaged in research on special educational needs on the condition that the researchers do not publish anything derived from or contained in the statement which would identify the child or parents concerned. School governing bodies should have access to a child's statement commensurate with their duties towards pupils with special educational needs and should always bear in mind the need to maintain confidentiality about the child in question.

4:76. Disclosure in the interests of the child also includes disclosure to any agencies other than the LEA who may be referred to in the statement as making educational or non-educational provision.

4:77. When the responsibility for a child with special needs changes from the LEA maintaining the statement (the old authority) to another LEA (the new authority), the old authority must transfer the statement to the new authority. They must also transfer any opinion they have received under the Disabled Persons (Services, Consultation and Representation) Act 1986 that the child is disabled. Upon the transfer of the statement, the new authority become responsible for maintaining the statement, and for providing the special educational provision specified in the statement.

4:78. The duty to maintain the child at the school specified in Part 4 of the statement therefore also transfers to the new authority. The new authority may place the child temporarily at a school other than that specified in Part 4 where appropriate and sensible to do so – for example, where the distance between the child's new home and the school would be too great – prior to the statement being amended in accordance with the statutory procedures. Otherwise, the new LEA may not decline to pay the fees or otherwise maintain the child at an independent school or non-maintained special school or a boarding school named in a statement, unless and until they have formally amended the statement.

4:79. The new authority may, on the transfer of the statement, bring forward the arrangements for the review of the statement, and may conduct a new assessment regardless of when the previous assessment took place. The new authority must tell the parents, within six weeks of the date of transfer, when they will review the statement and whether they propose to make an assessment under section 167. The old authority and the child's school should alert parents to the educational implications of their proposed move and both the old authority and the new authority should be ready to discuss those implications with parents. Where a child with a statement moves to Northern Ireland or Scotland, the LEA should, if the parent agrees, send a copy of the child's statement to the new authority or board.

Maintenance of a statement

4:80. When a statement is made, the LEA should tell the 'responsible person' in the child's school – see paragraph 2:9. The responsible person must then ensure that the child's special educational needs are made known to all those who will teach him or her. Schools should ensure that teachers monitor and informally review the child's progress during the course of the year. It is most important that, if a child's special educational needs change for the better or worse, a review is held as soon as possible to ensure that the provision specified in the statement is still appropriate.

5. Assessments and Statements for Under Fives

Introduction

5:1. Social services departments, district health authorities, NHS Trusts, Family Health Service Authorities and the voluntary sector already work very closely together with LEAs in many aspects of the planning and provision of services to under fives. LEAs should, wherever possible, use and build upon this well established network of relationships and services.

5:2. Young children should be assessed in a place where the child and family feel comfortable. Access to other parents and to family centres and other local services, play and opportunity groups and toy libraries may be important to the parents and to the child, and have a direct impact on the effective implementation of any assessment process or educational programme. The parental perspective is particularly important for children under five and the LEA should consider the use of parental guidelines on assessment to encourage parental participation.

5:3. LEAs should explain to parents of under fives with special educational needs their rights in relation to requesting a statutory assessment, and the implications of a statement – perhaps by issuing a leaflet.

Assessment of children under two

> **If an LEA believe that a child in their area who is under the age of two may have special educational needs for which the LEA should determine the special educational provision, the LEA may make an assessment of his or her educational needs if the parent consents to it, and must make such an assessment if the parent requests it. Such an assessment shall be in such manner as the authority consider appropriate. Following such an assessment, the LEA may make and maintain a statement of the child's special educational needs in such manner as they consider appropriate.**
>
> **(Section 175)**

5:4. When a child under two is referred to the LEA, it is probable that any special needs will have been first identified by his or her parents, the child health services or social services. The child is likely to have a particular condition or to have a major health problem which has caused concern at an early stage. Assessment of children under two need not follow the statutory procedures which are applicable to assessments of children who are aged two and over.

Statements for children under two

5:5. Statements will be rare for children under two. The LEA should first consider individual programmes of support according to the child's particular needs. The procedures are not specified in legislation. But, while LEAs may prefer to make voluntary agreements to cover such arrangements, they should be aware that a parental request for a statutory assessment could indicate that those arrangements are insufficient. For very young children LEAs should consider home-based programmes such as Portage (see Glossary) or peripatetic services for children with hearing or visual impairment. Parents should be consulted about the nature of the help and support which they would like to receive and some may prefer to attend a centre or to combine home-based with centre-based support.

5:6. If a decision is made to issue a statement, usually because of the child's complex needs or to allow access to a particular service such as a home-based teaching or a developmental play programme, it should include:

- **all available information about the child, with a clear specification of the child's special educational needs**
- **a record of the views of the parents and any relevant professionals**
- **a clear account of the services being offered, including the contribution of the education service and the educational objectives to be secured and the contribution of any statutory and voluntary agencies, and**
- **a description of the arrangements for monitoring and review.**

5:7. LEAs should ensure that any specific educational targets are regularly reviewed and, if necessary, revised. Any action will require close collaboration with child health services.

5:8. Careful monitoring of the child's progress should be a priority. LEAs should consider liaising with non-educational service providers for young children to ensure that record-keeping contains information relevant to identifying and meeting the child's special educational needs and to avoid duplication of investigations when the child is over two years.

Assessment of children under five

> **Those responsible for a school's governance (the LEA in the case of a maintained nursery school) shall use their best endeavours to secure that appropriate special educational provision is made for all their registered pupils with learning difficulties.**
> **(Section 161)**

5:9. The LEA may expect a nursery class or school to follow broadly the same procedures for identifying and meeting the special educational needs of children under five as Part 2 of this Code recommends for children of compulsory school age.

5:10. If the educational and/or developmental progress of the child under five gives rise to concern, the child's teacher, if the child is at school, should prepare a written report setting out the child's strengths and weaknesses and noting evidence for the concern. The use of parent assessment material and developmental checklists should be considered.

District Health Authorities (DHAs) and National Health Service (NHS) Trusts must inform the parents and the appropriate LEA when they form the opinion that a child under the age of five may have special educational needs. They must also inform the parents if they believe that a particular voluntary organisation is likely to be able to give the parents advice or assistance in connection with any special educational needs that the child may have.

(Section 176)

5:11. The child health services may alert the parents or school, where appropriate, to the child's potential difficulties. A child development centre or team will provide a multi-professional view at a very early stage. For children under five very early contact with child health services will be important in order to ensure that there is no physical cause for the difficulty in question (such as a hearing or visual impairment) or to secure advice on the possible cause and the effective management of difficult behaviour. Children's development and subsequent progress in school will also be affected by their general health status. All nursery classes and schools, playgroups (see Glossary) and opportunity playgroups should be aware of how to obtain information and advice on health related matters, using the school health service, the child's general practitioner or a relevant member of the child development centre or team, ensuring that parents are involved and can obtain as much help and advice as possible.

5:12. All services providing for young children, such as playgroups and day care facilities or other provision run by social services, child health services or voluntary organisations, should have information from the LEA on local procedures for the identification of special educational needs. Such information might incorporate an initial record form on which the child's key worker or service provider will set out the causes for concern and the views of any relevant people; confirm that the parents have been informed of the concern; and provide evidence that the child has been observed and that the request for assistance is firmly based. Social services departments have duties to register and to review day care arrangements in the statutory and voluntary sectors for children under eight. Liaison between the LEA and the relevant social services departments should ensure that there is clarity about how best to express concerns and about the information required in order to make such a referral positive and constructive.

5:13. Where a health authority or Trust (perhaps on the basis of information provided by a general practitioner) consider that a child might have special educational needs, they must inform the parents of their views and give the parents an opportunity to discuss those views with an officer of the health authority or Trust (usually a doctor who has appropriate knowledge and experience). They must then inform the relevant LEA.

5:14. Health authorities and Trusts must give parents the names of voluntary organisations which might be of assistance when they consider that a child under five may have special educational needs. The health services should give parents information on the full range of local statutory and voluntary services which might help them. Under the Children Act, local authority social services departments must produce written information on the full range of services in their area for children 'in need' and ensure that such information reaches those who might need it.

5:15. When a child under five is referred to the LEA by social services or the health services, there should be agreed procedures for acting speedily in order to ascertain whether the child's needs require specific intervention by the LEA. In the first instance the LEA may wish to invite a pre-school adviser or an educational psychologist to discuss with the service in question how best to take the matter forward. At this stage advice may be all that is required. In some instances referral to a child development centre or team may be the best way forward in order to clarify the nature of the child's difficulties. In other cases it may be clear that a child's difficulties warrant a statutory assessment.

Criteria for statutory assessment of children under five

5:16. When a child under five is already attending a maintained nursery school or class the LEA may expect that the broad principles of the school-based stages of assessment, action and review, adapted as appropriate in the light of the circumstances of the school concerned, will be followed as for older children. However, many young children will be attending provision made by social services, the health services or the voluntary or independent sectors when concern about a possible special educational need is first raised. Because early identification should lead to a more timely assessment and intervention which in turn should avoid the escalation of a difficulty into a significant special educational need, it is important that any concern about a child's development and progress should be shared at the earliest possible moment.

5:17. Staff working in non-educational settings for children under five may be uncertain about the basis for referral to the LEA and about the nature of the information or record keeping which would be most helpful in determining the best way forward for a particular child. Where referral for statutory assessment is made, the child will have demonstrated significant cause for concern. The LEA will seek evidence from the referring agency that any strategy or programme implemented for the child in question has been continued for a reasonable period of time without success, and that there is clear documentation of the child's difficulties and any action undertaken to deal with those difficulties.

5:18. In considering statutory assessment, the LEA should ask the following questions:

i.   where the child is at school, what difficulties have been identified by the school? Has the nursery class or school developed school-based strategies to assist the child?

ii. where the child is attending health services, social services, voluntary or private provision, have any concerns been raised about his or her development and has any outside advice been sought, regarding the child's:

- physical health and function
- communication skills
- perceptual and motor skills
- self-help skills
- social skills
- emotional and behavioural development
- responses to learning experiences?

5:19. The LEA will then assess the evidence and decide whether the child's difficulties or developmental delays are likely to be resolved only through a multi-professional approach which will require monitoring and review over a period of time.

Content of the statement for children under five

5:20. Where children between two and five have such complex needs that statutory procedures may be essential in order to maximise their opportunities, the statement will follow the same format as for any other children. The contributions of non-educational service providers are likely to be of key importance.

5:21. LEAs should note that parents of children under five may express a preference for a maintained school to be named in their child's statement and may make representations in favour of a non-maintained or independent school for their child. The LEA should ensure that parents have full information on the range of provision available within the authority and may wish to offer parents the opportunity to visit such provision and discuss any aspect of the provision with the Named Officer within the LEA. LEAs must provide parents with lists of independent schools approved under section 189 of the Act; all non-maintained special schools; and of all LEA-maintained and grant-maintained schools in the area of the LEA which cater for children of the appropriate age. They may also inform parents of such schools in neighbouring areas.

5:22. LEAs should informally review a statement for a child under five at least every six months to ensure that the provision is appropriate to the child's needs. Such reviews would complement the statutory duty to carry out an annual review in accordance with the Regulations but would not require the same range of documentation so long as they reflected the significant changes which can take place in the progress of a child under the age of five.

Special educational provision for children under five

5:23. For very young children, access to a home-based learning programme or the services of a peripatetic teacher for the hearing or visually impaired may provide the most appropriate help. In the case of a child with a behavioural difficulty, the advice of the clinical psychologist at a child development centre or an educational psychologist may enable the child to remain within an existing service. In some instances there may be a decision that a child should attend a nursery class or school (either within a mainstream or special school setting), playgroup or opportunity playgroup.

5:24. All services working within a local authority with young children, including home-based learning programmes, should have clearly articulated arrangements for access to their services. Those arrangements should be readily understandable by parents of children with special needs; indicate the kind of support which can be provided; and state any priority admission arrangements for such children.

5:25. The LEA should have information on nursery school or class places for children with special educational needs; and about places in play or opportunity groups, family centres, day nurseries or other provision for young children in that authority.

5:26. LEAs should consider the level of support which they can give to provision made through the voluntary sector and social services, such as playgroups and family centres. The under-fives forum or review groups which exist in many LEAs and which bring all statutory and relevant voluntary agencies together on a periodic basis offer useful opportunities to plan such collaborative approaches and to develop common criteria for the early identification and assessment of any special needs.

5:27. If a child is on a local authority child protection register, or where there is concern about a child's welfare, the LEA and social services department should consider jointly agreeing an arrangement for identifying a child's needs and specifying and monitoring the provision to meet such needs. If the child is looked after by the local authority – living with a foster parent or in a residential setting – the LEA's assessment could form part of the child's Child Care Plan and be regularly reviewed.

Moving to primary school

5:28. In some instances a child under five may have received considerable support without the necessity of making a statement. If it is decided that the child's needs are such that he or she will require a statement prior to entering primary school at five, careful attention should be paid to the parents' views and to information available from the full range of assessment arrangements within all the relevant agencies making provision for young children with special needs. Particular attention should be given to the child's general health and development and home environment to ensure that a learning difficulty is not directly related to wider family problems, and in order to provide appropriate support for the parents in making a full contribution to their child's progress at school.

5:29. All schools will wish to assess pupils' current levels of attainment on entry in order to ensure that they build upon the pattern of learning and experience already established during the child's pre-school years in nursery schools or classes, playgroups and other settings. Some LEAs operate 'multi-disciplinary under fives advisory panels', which give advice about a child's needs to the receiving primary school. If the child has an identified or potential special educational need, the head teacher, SEN coordinator and the child's class teacher should:

- **use information arising from the child's early years experience to provide starting points for the curricular development of the child**

- **identify and focus attention on the child's skills and highlight areas for early action to support the child within the class**

- **take appropriate action, for example developing an individual education plan, and monitoring and evaluation strategies to maximise development and alert any relevant support or external professionals at the earliest possible stage**

- **ensure that ongoing observation and assessment provide regular feedback to teachers and parents about a child's achievements and experiences and that the outcomes of such assessment form the basis for planning the next steps of a child's learning**

- **use the assessment process to allow children to show what they know, understand and can do, as well as to identify any learning difficulties**

- **involve parents in developing and implementing learning programmes at home and in school.**

5:30. The observations of a wide range of service providers for under fives will be invaluable in ensuring that schools can prepare an entry profile for children who may experience difficulties. LEAs should ensure that health, social services and the voluntary and independent sectors providing services for the under fives, as well as parents, fully understand the assessment and referral arrangements and that children's progress is carefully observed and recorded in order to inform any assessment procedure.

5:31. Children with a learning difficulty or developmental delay, and whose parents do not have English or Welsh as a first language are likely to be particularly disadvantaged if any special educational needs are not identified at the earliest possible stage. Parents may be unable to voice their own concerns because of lack of communication with the child's teacher or carer. LEAs should ensure that parents and relevant professionals are provided with access to interpreters and translated information material, so that early concerns may be shared about the child's behaviour, health and development. Bilingual support staff and teachers of English or Welsh as a second language may be able to help. Without such support early identification and intervention may be delayed or ineffective.

6. Annual Review

An LEA must review a statement within 12 months of making the statement or, as the case may be, of the previous review; and on making an assessment under section 167 of a child who already has a statement.

(Section 172(5))

Introduction

6:1. LEAs have the power to review a statement at any time during the year. LEAs should aim to secure the agreement of the school and the child's parents before exercising that power. LEAs must review all statements on an annual basis. The timing of annual reviews should reflect the circumstances of the child and the action which may flow from the review, for example about a move to secondary school. Timing should also reflect the circumstances of the child's school. Particularly in the case of special schools it may not be reasonable to review all statements at the same time at the end of the academic year. LEAs should seek to agree a reasonable spread of annual review dates with the school. Parents should always be informed.

6:2. The purpose of an annual review is to integrate a variety of perspectives on a child's progress, to ensure that he or she is achieving the desired outcomes and, if necessary, to amend the statement to reflect newly identified needs and provision. In some cases, the LEA will conclude that the statement's objectives have been secured and that they should cease to maintain the statement. The annual review should focus on what the child has achieved as well as on any difficulties which need to be resolved. While statements must be reviewed annually, schools, consulting parents and, as appropriate, the LEA, should, during the course of the year, monitor the child's progress towards the targets set out shortly after the statement was first made or at the last annual review.

6:3. The first annual review after the child's 14th birthday is particularly significant in preparing for his or her transition to the further education sector and adult life. Paragraphs 6:42–6:54 deal with procedures to be followed for that annual review. Paragraphs 6:6–6:41 deal with procedures for annual reviews in all other academic years.

6:4. The annual review should aim:

i. to assess the child's progress towards meeting the objectives specified in the statement and to collate and record information which the school and other professionals can use in planning their support for the child

ii. to assess the child's progress towards meeting the targets agreed following the making of the statement, in the case of the first annual review; and the targets set at the previous annual review, in the case of all other reviews

iii. to review the special provision made for the child, including the appropriateness of any special equipment provided, in the context of the National Curriculum and associated assessment and reporting arrangements. Where appropriate, the school should consider providing a profile of the child's current levels of attainment in basic literacy, numeracy and life skills, and a summary of progress achieved in other areas of the curriculum, including the National Curriculum. Where the statement involves a modification or disapplication of the National Curriculum, the school should indicate what special arrangements have been made for the child

iv. to consider the continuing appropriateness of the statement in the light of the child's performance during the previous year, and any additional special educational needs which may have become apparent in that time, and thus to consider whether to cease to maintain the statement or whether to make any amendments, including any further modifications or disapplication of the National Curriculum, and

v. if the statement is to be maintained, to set new targets for the coming year: progress towards those targets will be considered at the next annual review.

6:5. The child's circumstances may sometimes change during the year. He or she may have received education, for example, in a hospital school or in a pupil referral unit or through home tuition. Continuous assessment during the past year may have identified or confirmed a significant medical or social problem or learning difficulty which will require continuing support and intervention. The nature and outcomes of such provision should be addressed in the annual review and reports should be obtained from all those who have been involved in the child's educational progress during the preceding year.

The annual review for children at school

6:6. This section applies to all annual reviews except the first review to take place after the child's 14th birthday.

The LEA must require the head teacher of the child's school to submit a review report by a specified date. The LEA must give at least two months' notice of the date by which the report is required.

(Regulation 15(2))

> To prepare the review report, the head teacher must seek written advice from the parents, any people specified by the LEA, and from anyone else the head teacher considers appropriate. That advice will relate to the child's progress towards meeting the objectives in the statement and towards meeting any targets established to help meet the objectives specified in the statement; the application of the National Curriculum; the continued appropriateness of the statement; any Transition Plan (see paragraphs 6:45-6:47); any amendments to the statement; or whether the statement should cease to be maintained.
>
> **(Regulation 15(3) and (4))**

> Before producing the review report, the head teacher must convene a meeting to assist in its preparation. The head teacher must invite the parents and relevant staff member, any people specified by the LEA, and anyone else the head teacher considers appropriate; and must circulate copies of the advice received before the meeting. Following the meeting the head teacher must submit the review report to the LEA by the specified date.
>
> **(Regulation 15(5) and (10))**

6:7.   The LEA initiate the review. They conclude the process by considering a review report and recommendations prepared by the head teacher and then make their own recommendations, which they send to the school, the child's parents and all those invited to the review meeting. But most of the process is school-based, involving close cooperation between all concerned – the LEA, the child's school and parents, the child him or herself and other professionals.

6:8.   The head teacher can delegate to a teacher at the school any or all of the duties and functions prescribed to him or her in the Regulations. When such duties and functions are delegated, the head teacher should inform the LEA, the parents and anyone else involved in the review of the name of the teacher in question. The head teacher should ensure that the designated teacher is aware of all relevant representatives of the health services and the social services department and any individual professionals who should be invited to the review.

6:9.   The LEA must initiate the review by writing to the head teacher of the child's school, with a copy to the child's parents, asking the head teacher to:

■ **convene a review meeting and**

■ **prepare a review report**

6:10. The LEA must give the head teacher at least two months' notice of the date by which the review report must be returned to the LEA. The LEA must also tell the head teacher those whom he or she should invite to contribute to the review and to attend the review meeting. Those invited to the review meeting *must* include:

- **a representative of the LEA**

- **the child's parents, or, if the child is looked after by the local authority, his or her carer, and**

- **a relevant teacher, which may be the child's teacher or form/year tutor, the school's SEN coordinator, or some other person responsible for the provision of education for the child, the choice resting with the head teacher. In some schools, for example small schools, the functions of head teacher and relevant teacher may be fulfilled by one person.**

6:11. Where appropriate, the LEA *may* tell the head teacher that representatives of the health services or social services department or other professionals closely involved with the child must be invited to contribute to the review and attend the meeting. The head teacher may, of course, invite such representatives and professionals as he or she sees fit, even if not asked to do so by the LEA.

6:12. It is unlikely that all relevant professionals will be able to attend all review meetings. It may therefore be helpful when inviting them to indicate the priority attached to their attendance. Schools should explain to parents that professionals will not always be able to attend all review meetings and that, if beyond the review meeting, parents wish to discuss matters of concern in the professionals' reports, they should first approach the Named LEA Officer. Where a child is placed outside the LEA responsible for the statement, a representative of that LEA and relevant professionals such as educational psychologists should where possible attend the review meeting. Parents should be strongly encouraged to attend.

6:13. In preparing for the review meeting, the head teacher must:

- **request written advice from the child's parents, all those specified by the authority and anyone else the head teacher considers appropriate, and**

- **circulate a copy of all advice received to all those invited to the review meeting at least two weeks before the date of the meeting, inviting additional comments, including comments from those unable to attend the review meeting.**

6:14. District health authorities and social services authorities are required by section 166(1) of the Act to respond to the head teacher's request for written advice, unless the exceptions in section 166(2) and (3) apply. Other people from whom the head teacher requests written advice under Regulation 15(3) should also respond, although they are not under a statutory duty to do so. Head teachers must seek advice in accordance with Regulation 15(4). They are not required to seek advice on every one of those points from **all** the persons they ask for advice. Instead, head teachers can ask for specific advice from specific persons, or can ask for advice generally.

6:15. The evidence received, and comments on that evidence, together with an account of the review meeting, form the basis of the review report. Parents should be encouraged to contribute their views to the annual review process, to attend the review meeting, and to contribute to discussions about any proposals for new targets for the child's progress. Wherever possible, pupils should also be actively involved in the review process, including all or part of the review meeting, and should be encouraged to give their views of their progress during the previous year; discuss any difficulties encountered; and share their hopes and aspirations for the future.

6:16. Both parents and pupils may welcome assistance and advice in preparing their submissions and the LEA and school should be prepared to give assistance. Practical assistance with writing a report – such as recording and agreeing a discussion with an officer of the authority or a member of the school staff – may be helpful. Where parents or pupils seek independent support or guidance, referral to a relevant voluntary organisation may be helpful. Head teachers should tell parents and pupils that they may bring a friend, adviser, relative or their Named Person to the review meeting.

6:17. Where the parent or pupil wishes to discuss any aspect of the review process with the child's school or LEA, they should be encouraged to do so. Every effort should be made to inform parents of both their rights and their responsibilities and to encourage them to attend the review meeting. Where a parent does not respond to invitations to contribute in writing to the review, or to attend a review meeting, that information should be recorded in the review report with any reasons given.

6:18. When a child with special educational needs or his or her family does not have English or Welsh as a first language, the timescale for planning the annual review should take into account the need to:

- **translate any relevant documentation into the family's mother tongue**

- **ensure that interpreters are available to the child and family both in the preparatory stages to the review meeting and at the review meeting itself**

- **ensure that any professionals from the child's community have similar interpretation and translation facilities in order that they may contribute as fully as possible to the review process, and**

- **ensure that, where possible, a bilingual support teacher and/or teacher of English or Welsh as a second language is available to the child and family.**

6:19. Where a child or his or her family have a communication problem because of a sensory or physical impairment, similar attention should be given to the availability of all information and to representation at the review meeting through interpreters. Where alternative communication systems are used, the timing of the meeting should take into account the need to provide sufficient time for translation. Where a child or family has a visual impairment, similar attention should be given to the provision of all relevant information in Braille, large print or on tape as appropriate.

6:20. Where the child with a statement is subject to a care order, the local authority designated by the order will have parental responsibility (see Glossary) for that child. Such a child might be looked after by the local authority in a residential or foster placement, or might live at home. The extent of the contribution to be made by the child's parents and the child's carers – the residential social worker or foster parents – should be determined by the local authority in consultation with the social services department. If both the carers and the parents will be attending a review meeting, LEAs should consider involving social services in preparing parents and carers for the review and providing support before and after the review itself. Where the child with a statement is looked after by the local authority but is not subject to a care order, the child's parents still retain parental responsibility for that child.

6:21. Where a child is subject to a care order, an education supervision order, or is looked after by the local authority, the local authority social services department must include information on the arrangements for the education of the child within his or her Child Care Plan, as required under the Arrangements for Placement of Children Regulations made under the Children Act. The social services department must review the Child Care Plan and involve the child or young person in that process. As the Child Care Plan must include the educational arrangements for the child, LEAs and social services departments may wish to link the annual review of the statement with a review of the Child Care Plan in order to provide an integrated approach to meeting the child's needs.

Conduct of the review meeting

6:22. The review meeting will normally take place in the child's school and should be chaired by the head teacher or the teacher to whom responsibility for the school-based elements of the review has been delegated. The review meeting should address the following questions:

- **what are the parents' views of the past year's progress and their aspirations for the future?**

- **what are the pupil's views of the past year's progress and his or her aspirations for the future?**

- **what is the school's view of the child's progress over the past year? What has been the child's progress towards meeting the overall objectives in the statement? What success has the child achieved in meeting the targets set?**

- **have there been significant changes in the child's circumstances which affect his or her development and progress?**

- **is current provision, including the National Curriculum, or arrangements substituted for it, appropriate to the child's needs ?**

- **what educational targets should be adopted against which the child's educational progress will be assessed during the coming year and at the next review?**

- **is the Transition Plan – see paragraphs 6:45–6:47 – helping the pupil's progress to adult life?**

- **is any further action required and if so, by whom?**

- **does the statement remain appropriate?**

- **are any amendments to the statement required or should the LEA be recommended to cease to maintain it?**

6:23. The meeting should then make appropriate recommendations.

The annual review for children with statements whose education is otherwise than at school

6:24. When a child is educated otherwise than at school, the general timetable and arrangements for the annual review will remain the same as for children in schools. However, in these circumstances the LEA will convene the review meeting and the range of professionals involved may be wider and in some respects different from those involved in a school-based review. The child's parents must always be invited to the review meeting. The review meeting should take place in the most appropriate location, such as the LEA's offices or a hospital, and should normally be chaired by the LEA.

6:25. Where a child is educated otherwise than at school because of major difficulties relating to health or a disability, the views of the child's doctor should be sought. In such circumstances the attendance of professional advisers from the relevant child health services will be particularly important and the LEA should arrange the timing of the review meeting to ensure that they can, as far as possible, participate.

6:26. When a child has been excluded from school and is being educated either through home tuition or in a pupil referral unit, the views of the child's teacher and any other professionals who know the child and his or her strengths and weaknesses should be sought. Parents of children who have been excluded from school may need sensitive and positive encouragement to contribute to all stages of the review. They may wish to be accompanied to the review meeting by a friend, a relative, a professional or their Named Person. If the parent(s) and/or the child have a social worker, he or she may agree to undertake this role.

Action following annual reviews

6:27. Following the annual review meeting, the head teacher (or LEA if the child is being educated otherwise than at school) must prepare a report which summarises the outcomes of the review meeting and sets out any educational targets for the coming year, and must circulate this report to all concerned in the review, including the LEA, parents, pupils and any relevant professionals. Heads may find it helpful if LEAs were to offer guidance as to the form which reports should follow. This report must be circulated by the date specified by the LEA in their initial letter to the head teacher. The LEA must then review the statement, in the light of the review report and of any other information they consider relevant; make their own recommendations; if the child is aged over 15, make any necessary amendments to the Transition Plan (see paragraphs 6:45–6:47 below); and convey their recommendations and the amended Transition Plan to the child's school, parents and all those invited to the review meeting, before the statutory deadline for review.

6:28. A review meeting may recommend amendments to a statement if:

i.   significant new needs have emerged which are not recorded on the statement

ii. significant needs which are recorded on the statement are no longer present

iii. the provision should be amended to meet the child's changing needs and the targets specified at the review meeting or

iv. the child should change schools, either at the point of transfer between school phases, for example infant to junior or primary to secondary, or when a child's needs would more appropriately be met in a different school, for example by integration (see Glossary) in the mainstream.

6:29. The review meeting and the review report may also recommend that the LEA should cease to maintain the statement.

A change of school

6:30. All concerned with the child should give careful thought to transfer between phases. Advance planning is essential. The move should be considered at the review meeting during the child's last year in his or her current school. If necessary, that review should be brought forward to allow sufficient time for consideration of the school which will be appropriate for the child in the next phase. Arrangements for a child's placement should be finalised by the beginning of the child's last term before transfer. It is important for placements to be finalised as early as possible in order for any advance arrangements relating to that placement to be made and to ensure that parents feel confident and secure about the arrangements in question. Secondary and primary schools in an area should consider developing a common system of record-keeping to ease transfer of pupils between schools.

6:31. Under paragraph 8 of schedule 10 of the Act, parents have the right to request the LEA to substitute the name of a maintained, grant-maintained or grant-maintained special school for the name of the school in Part 4 of the statement. The LEA must comply with the request:

- **so long as it is made more than 12 months after**
  - **a similar request**
  - **the issue of a final copy of the statement**
  - **the issue of an amendment to the statement**
  - **the conclusion of an appeal to the SEN Tribunal over the provision specified in the statement,**

  whichever is the latest

- **and so long as**
  - **the school is suitable for the child, and**
  - **the child's attendance at the school would be compatible with the efficient education of other children already there and with the efficient use of resources.**

6:32. If these conditions apply, the LEA must amend the statement to name the school proposed by the parents and inform the parents, within eight weeks of receiving the request (Regulation 14(5)). Before naming the school, the LEA must first consult the governing body, and, if the school is maintained by another authority, that LEA. The eight week time limit allows for this consultation. The LEA may specify in the statement the date on which the child is to start attending the new school. That date might coincide with the start of a new term, or give sufficient time for the school to make necessary preparations for the child's arrival.

6:33. If the LEA conclude that they cannot name the school proposed by the parents, they must tell the parents, in writing, of their right to appeal to the Tribunal against the decision and should also explain why they have turned down the request. This letter should also be sent to the parents within eight weeks of their initial request (Regulation 14(5)). If the child is due to transfer between phases, the LEA must name a school which will be appropriate for that child. They should do so in the closest consultation with the child's parents and must follow the procedures for amending statements set out in paragraph 10 of schedule 10 to the Act.

Amending the statement

6:34. Where the LEA propose to amend a statement, whether to change the name of the school in Part 4 or for any other reason, they must write to the child's parents, informing them of that proposal and of their right to make representations within 15 days of the receipt of that proposal. LEAs should always explain the reasons for the proposal and ensure that the parents have copies of any evidence which prompted the proposal. A proposal to amend the statement will most often arise from the annual review: the parents should have already received copies of the review report and the LEA's recommendations.

6:35. The LEA must consider any representations made by the parents before deciding whether and how to amend the statement. If the authority conclude that an amendment should be made, they must make that amendment within eight weeks of sending the letter of proposal to the parents. They must also write to the parents informing them of the decision and the reasons for it; enclosing a copy of the amended statement and any relevant advice; and giving details of the parents' right of appeal to the Tribunal against the description in the statement of the child's special educational needs and the special educational provision, including the name of the school. If the LEA decide not to go ahead with the amendment, they should write to the parents explaining why, again within eight weeks of the original letter setting out the proposal to make an amendment.

Ceasing to maintain the statement

6:36. A statement will remain in force until the LEA ceases to maintain it, or until the child is no longer the responsibility of the LEA, for example, if he or she moves into the further or higher education sector, or to social services provision, in which case the statement will lapse. The LEA may cease to maintain a statement for a child only if they believe that it is no longer necessary to maintain it. The LEA must first write to the child's parents to give notice of their decision, and explain the parents' right of appeal to the Tribunal. The LEA should always explain their decision to the parents and ensure that the parents have copies of any evidence which has prompted that decision.

6:37. There should be no assumption that, once the LEA have made a statement, they should maintain that statement until they are no longer responsible for the young person. Statements should be maintained only when necessary: if the LEA conclude that they should cease to maintain a statement, any additional resources attached to it can be released to help other children. But a decision to cease to maintain a statement should be made only after careful consideration by the LEA of all the circumstances and after close consultation with the parents. The LEA should consider the results of recent annual reviews; should consider whether the objectives of the statement have been achieved; and should consider whether the child's needs could be met in future within the resources of mainstream schools within the area without the need for continuing LEA oversight. The LEA should always, therefore, consider whether, notwithstanding the achievement of some, or even all, of the objectives in the statement, the child's progress will be halted or reversed if the special educational provision specified in the statement or modified provision which justified the maintenance of a statement were not made.

Further statutory assessments

6:38. Under section 172 of the Act, the parents of a child with a statement may request a new assessment of that child under section 167 of the Act. The LEA must comply with such a request, so long as:

– no such assessment has been made within the previous six months, and

– the LEA conclude that it is necessary to make a further assessment.

6:39. The LEA must follow the procedures set out at paragraphs 3:17–3:21. The LEA should consider all such requests carefully. In particular they should consider whether there have been significant changes in the circumstances of the child. If the request for a further assessment originates from an annual review, much of the necessary information on which to base their decision will already be available to the LEA.

6:40. If the LEA conclude that a further assessment is not necessary, they must write to the parents, telling them of the decision and of their right to appeal to the Tribunal. The LEA should always give parents full reasons for their decision and should also write to the child's school. The LEA may wish to arrange a meeting between the parents and the school.

6:41. If the LEA decide that a further assessment is necessary, the procedures and time limits set out in Part 3 of this Code apply. Thereafter, if the LEA decide that they must amend the statement for the child, the procedures set out in paragraphs 6:34 and 6:35 apply. The resultant statement will supersede the previous statement.

Annual reviews from age 14–19

6:42. Some pupils with statements of special educational needs will remain in school after the age of 16. LEAs remain responsible for such pupils until they are 19. Others with statements will, however, leave school at 16, moving, for example, to a college within the further education sector or to social services provision. But, whatever the intended future destination of the young person, the annual review has an additional significance as he or she approaches the age of 16.

6:43. The first annual review after the young person's 14th birthday should involve the agencies who will play a major role during the post-school years. The transfer of relevant information should ensure that young people receive any necessary specialist help or support during their continuing education and vocational or occupational training after leaving school. For young people with disabilities, the role of social services departments will be of particular importance and local authorities have specific duties relating to other legislation which are set out below.

The first annual review after the young person's fourteenth birthday

6:44. The annual review procedure described above applies with the following exceptions:

- **the LEA convene the review meeting, even when the young person is at school. The LEA must invite the child's parents and relevant member of staff, any people specified by the head teacher, and anyone else the LEA consider appropriate**

- **the LEA must also ensure that other providers, such as social services, are aware of the annual review and the procedures to be followed, and must invite the social services department to attend the review so that any parallel assessments under the Disabled Persons Act (1986); the NHS and Community Care Act 1990; and the Chronically Sick and Disabled Persons Act 1970 can contribute to and draw information from the review process**

- **the LEA must invite the careers service to be represented at the review meeting, to enable all options for further education, careers and occupational training to be given serious consideration. The careers service will also be able to identify any specific targets which should be set as part of the annual review to ensure that independence training, personal and social skills, and other aspects of the wider curriculum are fully addressed during the young person's last years at school**

- **the LEA prepare the review report and the Transition Plan after the meeting, and circulate these to the young person's parents, the head teacher, all those from whom advice was sought, all those attending the review meeting and any others the LEA consider appropriate. In particular, the LEA should consider passing the review report and Transition Plan to the FEFC, particularly in cases where a decision might need to be taken about specialist college provision outside the further education sector (see also paragraphs 6:56–6:58).**

The Transition Plan

6:45. The first annual review after the young person's 14th birthday and any subsequent annual reviews until the child leaves school should include a **Transition Plan** which will draw together information from a range of individuals within and beyond the school in order to plan coherently for the young person's transition to adult life. Under sections 5 and 6 of the Disabled Persons Act 1986, at the first annual review after a child's 14th birthday LEAs must seek information from social services departments as to whether a child with a statement under Part III of the Education Act 1993 is disabled and may require services from the local authority when leaving school. LEAs should also consult child health services and any other professionals such as educational psychologists, therapists or occupational psychologists who may have a useful contribution to make.

6:46. The Transition Plan should address the following questions:

The School

■ What are the young person's curriculum needs during transition? How can the curriculum help the young person to play his or her role in the community; make use of leisure and recreational facilities; assume new roles in the family; develop new educational and vocational skills?

The Professionals

■ How can they develop close working relationships with colleagues in other agencies to ensure effective and coherent plans for the young person in transition?

■ Which new professionals need to be involved in planning for transition, for example occupational psychologists; a rehabilitation medicine specialist; occupational and other therapists?

■ Does the young person have any special health or welfare needs which will require planning and support from health and social services now or in the future?

■ Are assessment arrangements for transition clear, relevant and shared between all agencies concerned?

■ How can information best be transferred from children's to adult services to ensure a smooth transitional arrangement?

■ Where a young person requires a particular technological aid, do the arrangements for transition include appropriate training and arrangements for securing technological support?

■ Is education after the age of 16 appropriate, and if so, at school or at a college of further education?

The Family

■ What do parents expect of their son's or daughter's adult life?

■ What can they contribute in terms of helping their child develop personal and social skills, an adult life-style and acquire new skills?

■ Will parents experience new care needs and require practical help in terms of aids, adaptations or general support during these years?

The Young Person

■ What information do young people need in order to make informed choices?

■ What local arrangements exist to provide advocacy and advice if required?

■ How can young people be encouraged to contribute to their own Transition Plan and make positive decisions about the future?

■ If young people are living away from home or attending a residential school outside their own LEA, are there special issues relating to the location of services when they leave school which should be discussed in planning?

■ What are the young person's hopes and aspirations for the future, and how can these be met?

6:47. The Transition Plan should build on the conclusions reached and targets set at previous annual reviews, including the contributions of teachers responsible for careers education and guidance. It should focus on strengths as well as weaknesses and cover all aspects of the young person's development, allocating clear responsibility for different aspects of development to specific agencies and professionals. LEAs should advise schools on the proper balance of the transition programme components and ensure that all relevant information is available, together with advice and support as required. Social services departments, the health services and the careers service should be actively involved in the plan.

Involvement of social services departments

6:48. The first annual review after a child's 14th birthday will have a special significance because of the LEA's duties under sections 5 and 6 of the Disabled Persons (Services, Consultation and Representation) Act 1986. Sections 5 and 6 of that Act require LEAs to seek information from social services departments as to whether a child with a statement under Part III of the Education Act 1993 is disabled and may require services from the local authority when leaving school. The LEA must inform the appropriate and designated officer of the relevant social services department of the date of the child's first annual review after his or her 14th birthday and must similarly inform the social services department (if it is agreed that the child in question is disabled) between eight and 12 months before the expected school leaving date. LEAs may also inform social services departments at any time *after* the particular annual review required under section 5 of the Disabled Persons Act if it is considered that circumstances have changed and the young person concerned may now be considered to be disabled.

6:49. LEAs and, so far as is reasonable, schools should familiarise themselves with the following Acts, which may directly affect the future provision available to a young person with special educational needs:

The Chronically Sick and Disabled Persons Act 1970

The Employment and Training Act 1973 as amended by the Trade Union Reform and Employment Rights Act 1993

The Disabled Persons (Services, Consultation and Representation) Act 1986

The Children Act 1989

The National Health Service and Community Care Act 1990

The Further and Higher Education Act 1992

6:50. Under the Children Act 1989 and the NHS and Community Care Act 1990, social services departments are required to arrange a multi-disciplinary assessment and provide care plans for children and adults with significant special needs – which may include the provision of further education facilities.

6:51. The transition period may be associated with increasing levels of disability in some young people. It may therefore be necessary to plan for future increased special needs and for the provision of aids and adaptations both in a home and an educational setting. Young people may choose **not** to be assessed as disabled under sections 5 and 6 of the Disabled Persons Act and may similarly choose **not** to request help through the local authority community care arrangements. The LEA should give details of any relevant voluntary organisation or professional agency providing advice and counselling if such advice is needed. Schools should have information available on local sources of help and advice, including any local disability organisations which can provide information on the wider range of local services and offer independent advice and advocacy if required.

6:52. Local authority social services departments have duties under Section 24 of the Children Act 1989 to make arrangements for young people over 18 who are regarded as being 'in need' and who have been looked after by the local authority or received services from them prior to that date. LEAs should therefore ensure that the young person is aware of the power of the social services department to provide assistance beyond the age of 18 and provide any relevant information to the social services department in question in order to alert them of any potential special needs. Where a young person has been looked after in a foster placement or a residential home or attended a residential school outside his or her own local authority, the LEA should seek to ensure liaison between all relevant LEAs and social services departments.

The role of the careers service

6:53. The careers service must be invited to the first annual review following the young person's 14th birthday, and should also be invited to all subsequent annual reviews. Vocational guidance should be presented in the wider context of information on further education and training courses and should take fully into account the wishes and feelings of the young person concerned. The careers officer with specialist responsibilities should provide continuing oversight of, and information on, the young person's choice of provision, and assist the LEA and school in securing such provision and providing advice, counselling and support as appropriate. In some circumstances careers officers may also wish to involve occupational psychologists, who can contribute to the development of a vocational profile of a young person for whom future planning is giving cause for concern. Schools may in particular welcome guidance on curriculum development in independence, social or other skills, and ways of involving young people themselves in assessment and in strategies to address any behavioural or other problems which may otherwise adversely affect their further education or future employment.

6:54. Records of Achievement should be used, with the young person's consent, to provide information to colleges or any other provision to which the young person may move on leaving school. Where appropriate, Records of Achievement can be produced in Braille as well as in print, can make use of pictorial or abstract symbol systems, and may include a range of illustrative material (including supporting photographs, tapes or videos) which provide information on the young person.

Information

6:55. Circular 93/05 (B19/93 in Wales) from the Further Education Funding Council contains advice on the Council's arrangements for funding placements for students with learning difficulties and disabilities. It is the FEFC's responsibility in such circumstances to ensure that an assessment is made when such young people enter further education; in practice the LEA conducts the assessment on the FEFC's behalf in many cases. Circular 93/05 states that the assessment should be based upon:

- **the availability to young people and their advocates of a full range of information from the LEA about post-16 education and training choices, to inform placement decisions as indicated in the Parent's Charter**

- **the involvement of young people, their parents and their advocates in the assessment process, and**

- **the advice, wherever possible, of a range of professionals to ensure expert guidance, including for example careers officers, educational psychologists and other specialists who have knowledge of the individual's needs.**

Transfer to the further education sector

6:56. LEAs should ensure that where a young person has a statement of special educational needs, a copy of the statement together with a copy of the most recent annual review (together with any advice or information appended to it including the Transition Plan) should be passed to the social services department and the college or other provision that the young person will be attending. Where a decision might need to be taken by the FEFC about the placement of a student in a specialist college outside the FE sector, a copy of the Transition Plan should be sent to the FEFC. LEAs should seek the agreement of students and parents to the transfer of information (including statements) from school to the further education sector, but should explain the importance of such information and the desirability of the transfer.

6:57. Where students or their families consider that the information contained in the statement or annual review presents a negative picture or is inaccurate in some way, the LEA should consider how the review process can be made more positive and participative at the time of transition so that the conclusions of the last annual review are seen as an action plan for future development. The LEA should consider including in the review report information such as Records of Achievement which present the student in a positive light and provide information about his or her wider interests and abilities. The LEA should seek the consent of parents and students prior to the final annual review for the transfer of the review report and any Records of Achievement to the FEFC.

6:58. Schools should foster links with local further education colleges. This will help in the decision-making process and in the eventual transition itself, easing the move for both young person and staff at the further education college. Link provision with colleges can be of particular benefit to a young person with special educational needs by providing opportunities for integration, extending the curriculum and offering an induction into the adult environment of further education.

The involvement of young people in assessment and review

6:59. The views of young people themselves should be sought and recorded wherever possible in any assessment, reassessment or review during the years of transition. Some young people may wish to express these views through a trusted professional, family, independent advocate or adviser, the Named Person or through an officer of the authority. Effective arrangements for transition will involve young people themselves addressing issues of:

- **personal development**

- **self-advocacy**

- **the development of a positive self-image**

- **awareness of the implications of any long-term health problem or disability and**

- **the growth of personal autonomy and the acquisition of independent living skills.**

6:60. If the growth of these personal skills is to complement the student's progress through agreed academic and vocational curriculum arrangements and to inform choices about continuing education and future employment, student involvement on a regular basis in the annual review process should be encouraged.

Encouraging student involvement in decision-making during transition:

- **schools and LEAs should consider ways of ensuring that students' views are incorporated in planning for transition – for example the use of student counsellors, advocates or advisers, the Named Person, social workers or peer support**

- **curriculum planning should focus on activities which encourage students to review and reflect upon their own experiences and wishes and to formulate and articulate their views**

- **the student will need to come to terms with the wider implications of his or her disability or special need in adult life. Careful attention should be given to the avoidance of stigmatising language or labels and to the provision of accurate and sensitive advice and information on any aspects of the disability or special need as required**

- **transition should be seen as a continuum. Students should be encouraged to look to the future and plan how they will develop the academic, vocational, personal and social skills necessary to achieve their long-term objectives. Records of Achievement can demonstrate success and enable young people to recognise and value their own achievements as a contribution to their future learning and adult status and**

- **students will be most effectively involved in decision-making when supported by information, careers guidance, counselling, work experience and the opportunity to consider a wide range of options during the transition phase.**

Students without statements but with special educational needs

6:61. In some instances, a student approaching the age of 16 may have special educational needs which do not call for a statement, but which are likely to require some support if he or she goes on to further education. To ensure that these students are able to make decisions, and to facilitate their successful transition, it is important that they have appropriate help and guidance. This might include the provision of school/college link courses or work placements and should involve the different local agencies concerned. Further education colleges will need a thorough assessment of the young person's needs in order to make soundly based decisions about appropriate provision.

6:62. Schools providing support to students through the school-based stages of assessment should therefore consult as appropriate with other relevant services, such as the careers service, to ensure that relevant, detailed information is transferred to the FEFC, with the young person's consent. The LEA should provide schools with information on transition to the FE sector and details of local and national voluntary organisations which may help such students and their families. In some cases, schools may wish to prepare their own transition plans for students with special educational needs, but without a statement.

Appendix

Transitional Arrangements

1. Until 1 September 1994, the Education Act 1981 and the Education (Special Educational Needs) Regulations 1983, as amended and as made under the 1981 Act, will govern provision for children with special educational needs.

2. At 1 September 1994, the Education (Special Educational Needs) Regulations 1994, made under the Education Act 1993, come into effect. From that date, LEAs, governing bodies and those who assist them must have regard to this Code of Practice. Most provisions of the 1981 Act will be repealed.

3. Statements made under the 1981 Act and 1983 Regulations will remain valid legal documents under the new system. But to ensure a smooth transition between the old and new systems, some transitional arrangements are necessary. These arrangements apply to work in hand on assessments and statements at 1 September 1994; to the review of statements made before 1 September 1994; to statements transferred between authorities before 1 September 1994; and to the disclosure of statements. They are set out in regulation 21 of the 1994 Regulations.

4. In summary, Regulation 21 provides that:

   i. when, before 1 September 1994, an LEA have told parents that they are considering whether to make an assessment or have received a request from a parent for an assessment, the LEA must decide whether to make an assessment by 13 October 1994. If they do make an assessment, they must do so under the 1994 Regulations and within the time limits;
   (*Regulations 21(5) and 21(6)*)

   ii. where an authority are in the course of making an assessment under the 1983 Regulations at 1 September 1994, they will continue to make the assessment under those Regulations. If, however, they do not issue a proposed statement or tell parents that they will not make a statement by 1 January 1995, that assessment will lapse and a new assessment must be made under the 1994 Regulations and must be completed within ten weeks. Any relevant advice secured for the purpose of the 1983 Regulations assessment may be used to make the new assessment;
   (*Regulations 21(2) – 21(4)*)

   iii. where an authority have issued a proposed statement by 1 September 1994, that statement will be made under the 1983 Regulations;
   (*Regulation 21(7)*)

iv.   where, as a result of an assessment in train at 1 September 1994, the authority issue a proposed statement before 1 January 1995, that statement will be made under the 1983 Regulations;
(Regulation 21(7))

v.   the 1993 Act time limits on decisions to amend or cease to maintain a statement shall not apply where the relevant proposals were made before 1 September 1994;
(Regulation 21(8))

vi.   reviews which must be completed by 1 December 1994 will not be subject to the 1994 Regulations;
(Regulation 21(9))

vii.   when statements made under the 1983 Regulations are due to be reviewed on or after 1 December 1994, they must be reviewed with reference to the 1994 Regulations. But, as there may be no objectives specified in those statements and no arrangements specified for the setting of targets, one of the tasks of the first review will be to establish such objectives and set such targets, which will then be considered in subsequent reviews. In the case of a child aged over 14, the first review must also consider a Transition Plan. LEAs must set out the new objectives, targets and, as appropriate, the Transition Plan in writing when making recommendations as a result of the review of the statement. It will not, however, be necessary to amend the statement on this account although LEAs will be free to do so if they wish;
(Regulation 21(10))

viii. the 1981 Act and 1983 Regulations continue to apply to statements transferred before 1 September 1994, except that:

   a. when a statement has been transferred before 1 September and the receiving authority have not told parents whether they will make an assessment of the child, they must tell parents by 13 October 1994; and

   b. where a statement has been transferred before 1 September, the receiving authority must review the statement by 30 November 1994 or within a year of the date of the last review, whichever is the later;

   (Regulations 21(11) to 21(13))

ix.   statements made before 1 September 1994 may be disclosed for the purposes of appeals under the 1981 Act as well as any appeal under the 1993 Act.

   (Regulation 21(14))

5. Transitional arrangements governing appeals will be specified separately. The principle will be that the SEN Tribunal will hear appeals against decisions made by LEAs on or after 1 September 1994, whether those decisions were made in the light of the 1983 or the 1994 Regulations. Appeals against decisions made before that date, and hence in the light of the 1983 Regulations, will continue to be dealt with under the system established by the 1981 Act.

Glossary

These definitions relate to terms used in the Code. In the case of terms defined in legislation, the definitions given here are simplified and the full legal definitions can be found in the legislation referred to.

Annual review: the review of a statement of special educational needs which an LEA must make within 12 months of making the statement or, as the case may be, of the previous review.

Carer: for the purpose of this Code, a carer is a person named by a local authority to care for a child for whom the social services department has parental responsibility, ie a child who is the subject of a care order and who has been placed in a residential or foster placement. The carer may qualify as a parent for the purposes of the Education Acts because he or she has care of the child (see the definition of **Parent** below). If so, he or she will have a role to play in the consideration of a child's special educational needs.

Child protection register: in each area covered by a social services department, a central register must be maintained which lists all the children in the area who are considered to be suffering from, or are likely to suffer, significant harm and for which there is a child protection plan. This is not a register of children who have been abused but of children for whom there are currently unresolved child protection issues.

Children 'in need': a child is deemed to be 'in need':

– if he or she is unlikely, or does not have the opportunity to achieve or maintain a reasonable standard of health or development without provision made by the local authority; or

– his or her health and development are likely to be significantly impaired, or further impaired, without the provision of services by the local authority; or

– he or she is disabled. (Section 17(10), Children Act 1989)

Disapplication: removal or lifting of a programme of study, attainment target, assessment, or any other component of the National Curriculum, or any combination of these including entire subjects or the entire National Curriculum. (See also **Modification**, below.)

Education supervision order: an order that LEAs, under section 36 of the Children Act 1989, can apply for to put a child of statutory school age who is not being properly educated under the supervision of the LEA, with the intention of ensuring that he or she receives efficient full-time education suited to his or her age, aptitude, ability and any special educational needs, and that sufficient support, advice and guidance are provided to the parents.

Education Welfare Officer: person employed by an LEA to help parents and LEAs meet their respective statutory obligations in relation to school attendance. Education Welfare Officers also carry out related functions such as negotiating alternative educational provision for excluded pupils. In some LEAs Education Welfare Officers are known as Education Social Workers.

Funding Authority: the Education Act 1993 provides for the establishment of two funding authorities: in England, the Funding Agency for Schools (FAS), which was established on 1 April 1994; and in Wales, the Schools Funding Council for Wales (SFCW), which the Act empowers the Secretary of State for Wales to set up by Order. No Order has yet been made. The FAS is responsible for calculating and paying grant to grant-maintained and grant-maintained special schools and has responsibilities for the provision of school places in areas where there are significant numbers of grant-maintained schools. The SFCW, when established, will have similar responsibilities. Before the SFCW is set up, these functions will be carried out in Wales by the Secretary of State for Wales.

Independent school: a school neither maintained by a local education authority, nor a grant-maintained school, and which is registered under section 70 of the Education Act 1944. Section 189 of the Education Act 1993 sets out the conditions under which an independent school may be approved by the Secretary of State as being suitable for the admission of children with statements of special educational needs.

Information Technology (IT): covers a range of microcomputers, both portable and desktop; generic or integrated software packages, such as word processors, spreadsheets, databases and communication programmes; input devices such as keyboards, overlay keyboards, specialised access switches and touch screens; output devices such as monitors, printers and plotters; storage devices such as CD-ROM, and microelectronics controlled devices such as a floor turtle.

Integration: educating children with special educational needs together with children without special educational needs in mainstream schools wherever possible, and ensuring that children with special educational needs engage in the activities of the school together with children who do not have special educational needs.

Maintained school: for the purposes of this Code, any county school, grant-maintained school, grant-maintained special school, voluntary school or maintained special school.

Modification: amendment or alteration of a programme of study, attainment target, assessment or any other component of the National Curriculum in order to give the child access to that area of the Curriculum (see also **Disapplication**).

Named LEA Officer: the person from the LEA who liaises with the parents over all the arrangements relating to statutory assessment and the making of a statement. LEAs will inform parents of the identity of the Named Officer when they issue a notice of a proposal to make a statutory assessment of a child.

Named Person: the person whom the LEA must identify when sending the parents a final version of a statement. The Named Person, who should usually be identified in cooperation with the parents, must be someone who can give the parents information and advice about their child's special educational needs. He or she may be appointed at the start of the assessment process and can then attend meetings with parents and encourage parental participation throughout that process. The Named Person should normally be independent of the LEA and may be someone from a voluntary organisation or parent partnership scheme.

Note in lieu: a note issued to the child's parents and school when, following a statutory assessment, the LEA decide not to make a statement. The note should describe the child's special educational needs, explain why the LEA will not make a statement and make recommendations about appropriate provision for the child. All the advice received during the assessment should be attached to the note sent to the parents and, with their consent, should also be sent to the child's school.

Non-maintained special school: schools in England approved by the Secretary of State as special schools which are not maintained by the state but charge fees on a non-profit-making basis. Most non-maintained special schools are run by major charities or charitable trusts.

OFSTED – Office for Standards in Education / OHMCI – Office of Her Majesty's Chief Inspector (Wales): non-Ministerial government departments established under the Education (Schools) Act 1992 to take responsibility for the inspection of all schools in England and Wales respectively. Their professional arm is formed by Her Majesty's Inspectors (HMI).

Parent: this is defined in section 114 (1D) of the Education Act 1944, as amended by the Children Act 1989. Unless the context otherwise requires, parent in relation to a child or young person includes any person:

- who is not a natural parent of the child but who has parental responsibility for him or her, or

- who has care of the child.

Section 114(1F) of the 1944 Act states that for the purposes of sub-section (1D):

- parental responsibility has the same meaning as in the Children Act 1989, and

- in determining whether an individual has care of a child or young person any absence of the child or young person at a hospital or boarding school and any other temporary absence shall be disregarded.

Parental responsibility: under section 2 of the Children Act 1989, parental responsibility falls upon:

- all mothers and fathers who were married to each other at the time of the child's birth (including those who have since separated or divorced)

- mothers who were not married to the father at the time of the child's birth, and

- fathers who were not married to the mother at the time of the child's birth, but who have obtained parental responsibility either by agreement with the child's mother or through a court order.

Under section 12 of the Children Act 1989 where a court makes a residence order in favour of any person who is not the parent or guardian of the child that person has parental responsibility for the child while the residence order remains in force.

Under section 33(3) of the Children Act 1989, while a care order is in force with respect to a child, the social services department (SSD) designated by the order will have parental responsibility for that child, and will have the power (subject to certain provisions) to determine the extent to which a parent or guardian of the child may meet his or her parental responsibility for the child. The SSD cannot have parental responsibility for a child unless that child is the subject of a care order, except for very limited purposes where an emergency protection Order is in force under Section 44 of the Children Act 1989.

A person holding parental responsibility may make arrangements for another person to exercise that responsibility on his or her behalf – for example when the parent is on an extended visit abroad or during a time in hospital. This delegation does not remove the original parental responsibility. The Children Act introduced a concept of enduring parental responsibility (section 2(6)), which can only be removed through a court and which confers duties as well as rights on all those who have such responsibility.

Parental responsibility is defined under section 3(1) of the Children Act 1989 as covering all the duties, rights, powers, responsibilities and authority which parents have with respect to their children and their children's property.

Peripatetic teacher (or specialist, advisory, or support teacher): a teacher with specific expertise who travels from school to school and is employed by the LEA to give appropriate specialist advice and support to the child and the school. Often he or she will also teach children with special educational needs on a sessional basis, usually when an individual school does not justify the services of a full time teacher for the purpose.

Playgroups:

Sessional Playgroup: a group registered as sessional facilities or services, offering sessional care and education for children mainly aged three to five years of age cared for with or without parents, no single session lasting more than four hours and no main meal being provided by the group. Such groups are known under a variety of names, but they are all registered as playgroups.

Full and extended daycare playgroup: a group that accepts children under the age of five, without their parents, for more than four hours in any day.

Opportunity playgroup: a group that is set up primarily to provide for children with disabilities or learning difficulties alongside other children. The children often start at an earlier age than in a regular playgroup and staff usually have more specialised training in this field.

Parent and Toddler playgroup: a group of parents or carers with children under school age, most of the children below the age of three. These groups provide for both children and adults. Parents remain with the children throughout the session.

Portage: A planned approach to home-based pre-school education for children with developmental delay, disabilities or any other special educational needs. Portage began in Portage, Wisconsin, USA, and there is now an extensive Portage network in the UK, which is overseen by the National Portage Association.

Regional Organisations Expert in Information Technology for Communication Difficulties: the Aids to Communication (ACE) centres in Oxford and Oldham, the Centre for Micro-Assisted Communication at Charlton Park School, London SE7 and Communication Aids Centres funded under the NHS. Further information on these centres and on information technology for children with special educational needs may be obtained from the National Council for Educational Technology (NCET), Milburn Hill Road, Science Park, Coventry, CV4 7JJ. Telephone: 0203 416994.

Responsible Person: the head teacher or the appropriate governor, that is the chairman of the governing body unless the governing body have designated another governor for the purpose. In the case of a nursery school, the responsible person is the head teacher. The responsible person must be informed by the LEA when they conclude that a pupil at a school has special educational needs. The responsible person must then ensure that all those who will teach the child know about his or her special educational needs.

SCEA: the Service Children's Education Authority. The SCEA oversees the education of UK service children abroad. It is funded by the Ministry of Defence and operates its own schools as well as providing advice to parents on SCEA and UK schools.

SEN coordinator: member of staff of a school who has responsibility for coordinating SEN provision within that school. In a small school the head teacher or deputy may take on this role. In larger schools there may be an SEN coordinating team.

SEN Tribunal: an independent body established under the 1993 Act for determining appeals by parents against LEA decisions on assessments and statements. The Tribunal's decision will be binding on both parties to the appeal.

Special school: a school which is specially organised to make special educational provision for pupils with special educational needs and is for the time being approved by the Secretary of State under section 188 of the Education Act 1993.

Transitional arrangements: legal provisions which provide for a smooth change-over from the legal regime established by the Education Act 1981 and the Education (Special Educational Needs) Regulations 1983, to that established under the Education Act 1993 and the Education (Special Educational Needs) Regulations 1994.

Transition Plan: a plan which should form part of the first annual review after the child's 14th birthday, and any subsequent annual review. The purpose of the plan is to draw together information from a range of individuals within and beyond the school, in order to plan coherently for the young person's transition to adult life.

Welsh Language Act: advice on the Welsh Language Act and related matters can be obtained from the Welsh Language Board, Market Chambers, 5-7 St Mary Street, Cardiff, CF1 2AT.

Index

The Education (Special Educational Needs) Regulations 1994

These Regulations are not part of the Code of Practice,
but are appended to it for information

STATUTORY INSTRUMENTS

1994 No. 1047

EDUCATION, ENGLAND AND WALES

The Education (Special Educational Needs) Regulations 1994

Made 7 April 1994

Laid before Parliament 13 April 1994

Coming into force 1 September 1994

ARRANGEMENT OF REGULATIONS

PART I
General

PART II
Assessments

PART III

Statements

PART IV

Revocation and Transitional Provisions

SCHEDULE

In exercise of the powers conferred on the Secretary of State by sections 166(4), 168(2), 172(6), 301(6) of, and paragraphs 2 and 3 of Schedule 9 and paragraphs 5, 7, and 8 of Schedule 10 to the Education Act 1993(**a**), and by section 19 and paragraphs 1 and 3 of Schedule 1 to the Education Act 1981(**b**) the Secretary of State for Education, as respects England, and the Secretary of State for Wales, as respects Wales, hereby make the following Regulations:

(a)   1993 c.35.

(b)   1981 c.60.

PART I

GENERAL

Title and commencement

1.   These Regulations may be cited as the Education (Special Educational Needs) Regulations 1994 and shall come into force on 1st September 1994.

Interpretation

2. —(1)   In these Regulations —

'the Act' means the Education Act 1993;

'authority' means a local education authority;

'district health authority' has the same meaning as in the National Health Service Act 1977(**c**);

'head teacher' includes any person to whom the duties or functions of a head teacher under these Regulations have been delegated by the head teacher in accordance with regulation 3;

'social services authority' means a local authority for the purposes of the Local Authority Social Services Act 1970(**d**) acting in the discharge of such functions as are referred to in section 2(1) of that Act;

'target' means the knowledge, skills and understanding which a child is expected to have by the end of a particular period;

'transition plan' means a document prepared pursuant to regulation 16(9) or 17(9) which sets out the arrangements which an authority consider appropriate for a young person during the period when he is aged 14 to 19 years, including arrangements for special educational provision and for any other necessary provision, for suitable employment and accommodation and for leisure activities, and which will facilitate a satisfactory transition from childhood to adulthood;

'working day' means a day other than a Saturday, Sunday, Christmas Day, Good Friday or Bank Holiday within the meaning of the Banking and Financial Dealings Act 1971(**e**);

(c)   1977 c.49; section 8 was amended by paragraph 28 of Schedule 1 to the Health Services Act 1980 (c.53) and by sections 1(1) of and Schedule 10 to the National Health Service and Community Care Act 1990 (c.19); the definition of 'district health authority' in section 128(1) was substituted by section 26(1) and (2)(b) of the National Health Service and Community Care Act 1990.

(d)   1970 c.42; section 1 was amended by section 195(1) of the Local Government Act 1972 (c.70).

(e)   1971 c.80.

'the 1981 Act' means the Education Act 1981(**f**);

'the 1983 Regulations' means the Education (Special Educational Needs) Regulations 1983(**g**).

(2) In these Regulations any reference to the district health authority or the social services authority is, in relation to a particular child, a reference to the district health authority or social services authority in whose area that child lives.

(3) Where a thing is required to be done under these Regulations –

    (a) within a period after an action is taken, the day on which that action was taken shall not be counted in the calculation of that period; and

    (b) within a period and the last day of that period is not a working day, the period shall be extended to include the following working day.

(4) References in these Regulations to a section are references to a section of the Act.

(5) References in these Regulations to a regulation are references to a regulation in these Regulations and references to a Schedule are references to the Schedule to these Regulations.

Delegation of functions

3. Where a head teacher has any functions or duties under these Regulations he may delegate those functions or duties –

    (a) generally to a member of the staff of the school who is a qualified teacher, or

    (b) in a particular case to a member of the staff of the school who teaches the child in question.

Service of documents

4. –(1) Where any provision in Part III of the Act or in these Regulations authorises or requires any document to be served on or sent to a person or any written notice to be given to a person the document may be served or sent or the notice may be given by properly addressing, pre-paying and posting a letter containing the document or notice.

(2) For the purposes of this regulation, the proper address of a person is –

    (a) in the case of the child's parent, his last known address;

    (b) in the case of a head teacher or other member of the staff of a school, the school's address;

(f) 1981 c.60.

(g) S.I. 1983/29, amended by S.I. 1988/1067 and 1990/1524.

(c) in the case of any other person, the last known address of the place where he carries on his business, profession or other employment.

(3) Where first class post is used, the document or notice shall be treated as served, sent or given on the second working day after the date of posting, unless the contrary is shown.

(4) Where second class post is used, the document or notice shall be treated as served, sent or given on the fourth working day after the date of posting, unless the contrary is shown.

(5) The date of posting shall be presumed, unless the contrary is shown, to be the date shown in the post-mark on the envelope in which the document is contained.

PART II
ASSESSMENTS

Notices relating to assessment

5. −(1) Where under section 167(1) or 174(2) an authority give notice to a child's parent that they propose to make an assessment, or under section 167(4) give notice to a child's parent of their decision to make an assessment, they shall send copies of the relevant notice to −

(a) the social services authority,

(b) the district health authority, and

(c) if the child is registered at a school, the head teacher of that school.

(2) Where a copy of a notice is sent under paragraph (1) an endorsement on the copy or a notice accompanying that copy shall inform the recipient what help the authority are likely to request.

(3) Where under section 172(2) or 173(1) a child's parent asks the authority to arrange for an assessment to be made the authority shall give notice in writing to the persons referred to in paragraph (1)(a) to (c) of the fact that the request has been made and inform them what help they are likely to request.

Advice to be sought

6. −(1) For the purpose of making an assessment under section 167 an authority shall seek −

(a) advice from the child's parent;

(b) educational advice as provided for in regulation 7;

(c) medical advice from the district health authority as provided for in regulation 8;

(d) psychological advice as provided for in regulation 9;

(e) advice from the social services authority; and

(f) any other advice which the authority consider appropriate for the purpose of arriving at a satisfactory assessment.

(2) The advice referred to in paragraph (1) shall be written advice relating to –

(a) the educational, medical, psychological or other features of the case (according to the nature of the advice sought) which appear to be relevant to the child's educational needs (including his likely future needs);

(b) how those features could affect the child's educational needs, and

(c) the provision which is appropriate for the child in light of those features of the child's case, whether by way of special educational provision or non-educational provision, but not relating to any matter which is required to be specified in a statement by virtue of section 168(4)(b).

(3) A person from whom the advice referred to in paragraph (1) is sought may in connection therewith consult such persons as it appears to him expedient to consult; and he shall consult such persons, if any, as are specified in the particular case by the authority as persons who have relevant knowledge of, or information relating to, the child.

(4) When seeking the advice referred to in paragraph (1)(b) to (f) an authority shall provide the person from whom it is sought with copies of –

(a) any representations made by the parent, and

(b) any evidence submitted by, or at the request of, the parent under section 167(1)(d).

(5) The authority need not seek the advice referred to in paragraph (1)(b), (c), (d), (e) or (f) if –

(a) the authority have obtained advice under paragraph (1)(b), (c), (d), (e) or (f) respectively within the preceding 12 months, and

(b) the authority, the person from whom the advice was obtained and the child's parent are satisfied that the existing advice is sufficient for the purpose of arriving at a satisfactory assessment.

Educational advice

7. –(1) The educational advice referred to in regulation 6(1)(b) shall, subject to paragraphs (2) to (5), be sought –

(a) from the head teacher of each school which the child is currently attending or which he has attended at any time within the preceding 18 months;

(b) if advice cannot be obtained from a head teacher of a school which the child is currently attending (because the child is not attending a school or otherwise) from a person who the authority are satisfied has experience of teaching children with special educational needs or knowledge of the differing provision which may be called for in different cases to meet those needs;

(c) if the child is not currently attending a school and if advice obtained under subparagraph (b) is not advice from such a person, from a person responsible for educational provision for him; and

(d) if any of the child's parents is a serving member of Her Majesty's armed forces, from the Service Children's Education Authority.

(2) The advice sought as provided in paragraph (1) shall not be sought from any person who is not a qualified teacher within the meaning of section 218 of the Education Reform Act 1988(**h**).

(3) The advice sought from a head teacher as provided in paragraph (1)(a) shall, if the head teacher has not himself taught the child within the preceding 18 months, be advice given after consultation with a teacher who has so taught the child.

(4) The advice sought from a head teacher as provided in paragraph (1)(a) shall include advice relating to the steps which have been taken by the school to identify and assess the special educational needs of the child and to make provision for the purpose of meeting those needs.

(5) Where it appears to the authority, in consequence of medical advice or otherwise, that the child in question is –

(a) hearing impaired, or

(b) visually impaired, or

(c) both hearing impaired and visually impaired,

and any person from whom advice is sought as provided in paragraph (1) is not qualified to teach pupils who are so impaired then the advice sought shall be advice given after consultation with a person who is so qualified.

(6) For the purposes of paragraph (5) a person shall be considered to be qualified to teach pupils who are hearing impaired or visually impaired or who are both hearing impaired and visually impaired if he is qualified to be employed at a school as a teacher of a class for pupils who are so impaired otherwise than to give instruction in a craft, trade, or domestic subject.

(7) Paragraphs (3) and (5) are without prejudice to regulation 6(3).

Medical advice

8.   The advice referred to in paragraph 6(1)(c) shall be sought from the district health authority, who shall obtain the advice from a fully registered medical practitioner.

(h)   1988 c.40.

Psychological advice

9. −(1) The psychological advice referred to in regulation 6(1)(d) shall be sought from a person −

(a) regularly employed by the authority as an educational psychologist, or

(b) engaged by the authority as an educational psychologist in the case in question.

(2) The advice sought from a person as provided in paragraph (1) shall, if that person has reason to believe that another psychologist has relevant knowledge of, or information relating to, the child, be advice given after consultation with that other psychologist.

(3) Paragraph (2) is without prejudice to regulation 6(3).

Matters to be taken into account in making an assessment

10. When making an assessment an authority shall take into consideration −

(a) any representations made by the child's parent under section 167(1)(d);

(b) any evidence submitted by, or at the request of, the child's parent under section 167(1)(d); and

(c) the advice obtained under regulation 6.

Time limits

11.−(1) Where under section 167(1) the authority serve a notice on the child's parent informing him that they propose to make an assessment of the child's educational needs under section 167 they shall within 6 weeks of the date of service of the notice give notice to the child's parent −

(a) under section 167(4) of their decision to make an assessment, and of their reasons for making that decision, or

(b) under section 167(6) of their decision not to assess the educational needs of the child.

(2) Where under section 174(2) the authority serve a notice on the child's parent informing him that they propose to make an assessment of the child's educational needs under section 167 they shall within 6 weeks of the date of service of the notice give notice to the child's parent and to the governing body of the grant-maintained school which asked the authority to make an assessment−

(a) under section 174(5) of their decision to make an assessment and their reasons for making that decision, or

(b) under section 174(6) of their decision not to assess the educational needs of the child.

(3) Where under sections 172(2) or 173(1) a parent asks the authority to arrange for an assessment to be made under section 167 they shall within 6 weeks of the date of receipt of the request give notice to the child's parent –

(a) under section 167(4) of their decision to make an assessment, or

(b) under section 172(3)(a) or 173(2)(a) respectively of their decision not to comply with the request and of the parent's right to appeal to the Tribunal against the determination.

(4) An authority need not comply with the time limits referred to in paragraphs (1) to (3) if it is impractical to do so because –

(a) the authority have requested advice from the head teacher of a school during a period beginning one week before any date on which that school was closed for a continuous period of not less than 4 weeks from that date and ending one week before the date on which it re-opens;

(b) exceptional personal circumstances affect the child or his parent during the 6 week period referred to in paragraphs (1) to (3); or

(c) the child or his parent are absent from the area of the authority for a continuous period of not less than 4 weeks during the 6 week period referred to in paragraphs (1) to (3).

(5) Subject to paragraph (6), where under section 167(4) an authority have given notice to the child's parent of their decision to make an assessment they shall complete that assessment within 10 weeks of the date on which such notice was given.

(6) An authority need not comply with the time limit referred to in paragraph (5) if it is impractical to do so because –

(a) in exceptional cases after receiving advice sought under regulation 6 it is necessary for the authority to seek further advice;

(b) the child's parent has indicated to the authority that he wishes to provide advice to the authority after the expiry of 6 weeks from the date on which a request for such advice under regulation 6(a) was received, and the authority have agreed to consider such advice before completing the assessment;

(c) the authority have requested advice from the head teacher of a school under regulation 6(1)(b) during a period beginning one week before any date on which that school was closed for a continuous period of not less than 4 weeks from that date and ending one week before the date on which it re-opens;

(d) the authority have requested advice from a district health authority or a social services authority under regulation 6(1)(c) or (e) respectively and the district health authority or the social services authority have not complied with that request within 6 weeks from the date on which it was made;

(e) exceptional personal circumstances affect the child or his parent during the 10 week period referred to in paragraph (5);

(f) the child or his parent are absent from the area of the authority for a continuous period of not less than 4 weeks during the 10 week period referred to in paragraph (5); or

(g) the child fails to keep an appointment for an examination or a test during the 10 week period referred to in paragraph (5).

(7) Subject to paragraph (8), where an authority have requested advice from a district health authority or a social services authority under regulation 6(1)(c) or (e) respectively they shall comply with that request within 6 weeks of the date on which they receive it.

(8) A district health authority or a social services authority need not comply with the time limit referred to in paragraph (7) if it is impractical to do so because –

(a) exceptional personal circumstances affect the child or his parent during the 6 week period referred to in paragraph (7);

(b) the child or his parent are absent from the area of the authority for a continuous period of not less than 4 weeks during the 6 week period referred to in paragraph (7);

(c) the child fails to keep an appointment for an examination or a test made by the district health authority or the social services authority respectively during the 6 week period referred to in paragraph (7); or

(d) they have not before the date on which a copy of a notice has been served on them in accordance with regulation 5(1) or a notice has been served on them in accordance with regulation 5(3) produced or maintained any information or records relevant to the assessment of the child under section 167.

PART III

STATEMENTS

Notice accompanying a proposed statement

12. The notice which shall accompany a copy of a proposed statement served on the parent pursuant to paragraph 2 of Schedule 10 to the Act shall be in a form substantially corresponding to that set out in Part A of the Schedule and shall contain the information therein specified.

Statement of special educational needs

13. A statement of a child's special educational needs made under section 168(1) shall be in a form substantially corresponding to that set out in Part B of the

Schedule, shall contain the information therein specified, and shall be dated and authenticated by the signature of a duly authorised officer of the authority concerned.

Time limits

14.–(1) Where under section 167 an authority have made an assessment of the educational needs of a child for whom no statement is maintained they shall within two weeks of the date on which the assessment was completed either –

(a) serve a copy of a proposed statement and a written notice on the child's parent under paragraph 2 of Schedule 10 to the Act, or

(b) give notice in writing to the child's parent under section 169(1) that they have decided not to make a statement and that he may appeal against that decision to the Tribunal.

(2) Where under section 167 an authority have made an assessment of the educational needs of a child for whom a statement is maintained they shall within two weeks of the date on which the assessment was completed –

(a) under paragraph 10(1) of Schedule 10 to the Act serve on the child's parent a notice that they propose to amend the statement and of his right to make representations;

(b) under paragraph 11(2) of Schedule 10 to the Act give notice to the child's parent that they have determined to cease to maintain the statement and of his right of appeal to the Tribunal; or

(c) serve on the child's parent a notice which informs him that they have determined not to amend the statement and their reasons for that determination, which is accompanied by copies of the professional advice obtained during the assessment, and which informs the child's parent that under section 170(1)(c) he may appeal to the Tribunal against the description in the statement of the authority's assessment of the child's special educational needs, the special educational provision specified in the statement or, if no school is named in the statement, that fact.

(3) Subject to paragraph (4), where an authority have served a copy of a proposed statement on the child's parent under paragraph 2 of Schedule 10 to the Act they shall within 8 weeks of the date on which the proposed statement was served serve a copy of the completed statement and a written notice on the child's parent under paragraph 6 of that Schedule, or give notice to the child's parent that they have decided not to make a statement.

(4) The authority need not comply with the time limit referred to in paragraph (3) if it is impractical to do so because –

(a) exceptional personal circumstances affect the child or his parent during the 8 week period referred to in paragraph (3);

(b) the child or his parent are absent from the area of the authority for a continuous period of not less than 4 weeks during the 8 week period referred to in paragraph (3);

(c) the child's parent indicates that he wishes to make representations to the authority about the content of the statement under paragraph 4(1)(a) of Schedule 10 to the Act after the expiry of the 15 day period for making such representations provided for in paragraph 4(4) of that Schedule;

(d) a meeting between the child's parent and an officer of the authority has been held pursuant to paragraph 4(1)(b) of Schedule 10 to the Act and the child's parent has required that another such meeting be arranged or under paragraph 4(2) of that Schedule has required a meeting with the appropriate person under to be arranged; or

(e) the authority have sent a written request to the Secretary of State seeking his consent under section 189(5)(b) to the child being educated at an independent school which is not approved by him and such consent has not been received by the authority within two weeks of the date on which the request was sent.

(5) Where under paragraph 8(1) of Schedule 10 to the Act the child's parent asks the authority to substitute for the name of a school or institution specified in a statement the name of another school specified by him and where the condition referred to in paragraph 8(1)(b) of that Schedule has been satisfied the authority shall within 8 weeks of the date on which the request was received either –

(a) comply with the request; or

(b) give notice to the child's parent under paragraph 8(3) of that Schedule that they have determined not to comply with the request and that he may appeal against that determination to the Tribunal.

(6) Where under paragraph 10(1) of Schedule 10 to the Act an authority serve a notice on the child's parent informing him of their proposal to amend a statement they shall not amend the statement after the expiry of 8 weeks from the date on which the notice was served.

(7) Where under paragraph 11(2) of Schedule 10 to the Act an authority give notice to the child's parent that they have determined to cease to maintain a statement they shall not cease to maintain the statement –

(a) before the expiry of the prescribed period during which the parent may appeal to the Tribunal against the determination, or

(b) after the expiry of 4 weeks from the end of that period.

Review of statement where child not aged 14 attends school

15.–(1) This regulation applies where –

(a) an authority review a statement under section 172(5) other than on the making of an assessment,

(b) the child concerned attends a school, and

(c) regulation 16 does not apply.

(2) The authority shall by notice in writing require the head teacher of the child's school to submit a report to them under this regulation by a specified date not less than two months from the date the notice is given and shall send a copy of the notice to the child's parent.

(3) The head teacher shall for the purpose of preparing the report referred to in paragraph (2) seek advice as to the matters referred to in paragraph (4) from –

(a) the child's parent;

(b) any person whose advice the authority consider appropriate for the purpose of arriving at a satisfactory report and whom they specify in the notice referred to in paragraph (2), and

(c) any person whose advice the head teacher considers appropriate for the purpose of arriving at a satisfactory report.

(4) The advice referred to in paragraph (3) shall be written advice as to –

(a) the child's progress towards meeting the objectives specified in the statement;

(b) the child's progress towards attaining any targets established in furtherance of the objectives specified in the statement;

(c) where the school is not established in a hospital and is a maintained, grant-maintained or grant-maintained special school, the application of the provisions of the National Curriculum to the child;

(d) where the school is not established in a hospital and is a maintained, grant-maintained or grant-maintained special school, the application of any provisions substituted for the provisions of the National Curriculum in order to maintain a balanced and broadly based curriculum;

(e) where appropriate, and in any case where a transition plan exists, any matters which are the appropriate subject of such a plan;

(f) whether the statement continues to be appropriate;

(g) any amendments to the statement which would be appropriate; and

(h) whether the authority should cease to maintain the statement.

(5) The notice referred to in paragraph (2) shall require the head teacher to invite the following persons to attend a meeting to be held on a date before the report referred to in that paragraph is submitted –

(a) the representative of the authority specified in the notice,

(b) the child's parent,

(c) a member or members of the staff of the school who teach the child or who are otherwise responsible for the provision of education for the child whose attendance the head teacher considers appropriate,

(d) any other person whose attendance the head teacher considers appropriate, and

(e) any person whose attendance the authority consider appropriate and who is specified in the notice.

(6) The head teacher shall not later than two weeks before the date on which a meeting referred to in paragraph (5) is to be held send to all the persons invited to that meeting copies of the advice he has received pursuant to his request under paragraph (3) and by written notice accompanying the copies shall request the recipients to submit to him before or at the meeting written comments on that advice and any other advice which they think appropriate.

(7) The meeting referred to in paragraph (5) shall consider –

(a) the matters referred to in paragraph (4); and

(b) any significant changes in the child's circumstances since the date on which the statement was made or last reviewed.

(8) The meeting shall recommend –

(a) any steps which it concludes ought to be taken, including whether the authority should amend or cease to maintain the statement,

(b) any targets to be established in furtherance of the objectives specified in the statement which it concludes the child ought to meet during the period until the next review, and

(c) where a transition plan exists, the matters which it concludes ought to be included in that plan.

(9) If the meeting cannot agree the recommendations to be made under paragraph (8) the persons who attended the meeting shall make differing recommendations as appears necessary to each of them.

(10) The report to be submitted under paragraph (2) shall be completed after the meeting is held and shall include the head teacher's assessment of the matters referred to in paragraph (7) and his recommendations as to the matters referred to in paragraph (8), and shall refer to any difference between his assessment and recommendations and those of the meeting.

(11) When the head teacher submits his report to the authority under paragraph (2) he shall at the same time send copies to –

(a) the child's parent,

(b) the persons from whom the head teacher sought advice under paragraph (3),

(c) the persons who were invited to attend the meeting in accordance with paragraph (5),

(d) any other person to whom the authority consider it appropriate that a copy be sent and to whom they direct him to send a copy, and

(e) any other person to whom the head teacher considers it appropriate that a copy be sent.

(12) The authority shall review the statement under section 172(5) in light of the report and any other information or advice which they consider relevant, shall make written recommendations as to the matters referred to in paragraph (8)(a) and (b) and, where a transition plan exists, shall amend the plan as they consider appropriate.

(13) The authority shall within one week of completing the review under section 172(5) send copies of the recommendations and any transition plan referred to in paragraph (12) to –

(a) the child's parent;

(b) the head teacher;

(c) the persons from whom the head teacher sought advice under paragraph (3);

(d) the persons who were invited to attend the meeting in accordance with paragraph (5), and

(e) any other person to whom the authority consider it appropriate that a copy be sent.

Review of statement where child aged 14 attends school

16.–(1) This regulation applies where –

(a) an authority review a statement under section 172(5) other than on the making of an assessment,

(b) the child concerned attends a school, and

(c) the review is the first review commenced after the child has attained the age of 14 years.

(2) The authority shall for the purpose of preparing a report under this regulation by notice in writing require the head teacher of the child's school to seek the advice referred to in regulation 15(4), including in all cases advice as to the matters referred to in regulation 15(4)(e), from –

(a) the child's parent,

(b) any person whose advice the authority consider appropriate for the purpose of arriving at a satisfactory report and whom they specify in the notice referred to above, and

(c) any person whose advice the head teacher considers appropriate for the purpose of arriving at a satisfactory report.

(3) The authority shall invite the following persons to attend a meeting to be held on a date before the review referred to in paragraph (1) is required to be completed–

(a) the child's parent;

(b) a member or members of the staff of the school who teach the child or who are otherwise responsible for the provision of education for the child whose attendance the head teacher considers appropriate and whom he has asked the authority to invite;

(c) a representative of the social services authority;

(d) a person providing careers services under sections 8 to 10 of the Employment and Training Act 1973 **(i)**;

(e) any person whose attendance the head teacher considers appropriate and whom he has asked the authority to invite; and

(f) any person whose attendance the authority consider appropriate.

(4) The head teacher shall not later than two weeks before the date on which the meeting referred to in paragraph (3) is to be held serve on all the persons invited to attend that meeting copies of the advice he has received pursuant to his request under paragraph (2) and shall by written notice request the recipients to submit to him before or at the meeting written comments on that advice and any other advice which they think appropriate.

(5) A representative of the authority shall attend the meeting.

(6) The meeting shall consider the matters referred to in regulation 15(7), in all cases including the matters referred to in regulation 15(4)(e), and shall make recommendations in accordance with regulation 15(8) and (9), in all cases including recommendations as to the matters referred to in regulation 15(8)(c).

(7) The report to be prepared by the authority under paragraph (2) shall be completed after the meeting, shall contain the authority's assessment of the matters required to be considered by the meeting and their recommendations as to the matters required to be recommended by it and shall refer to any difference between their assessment and recommendations and those of the meeting.

(8) The authority shall within one week of the date on which the meeting was held send copies of the report completed under paragraph (7) to –

(a) the child's parent;

(b) the head teacher;

(c) the persons from whom the head teacher sought advice under paragraph (2);

(d) the persons who were invited to attend the meeting under paragraph (3); and

---

(i) 1973 c.50. Sections 8 to 10 were replaced by section 45 of the Trade Union and Employment Rights Act 1993 (c.19).

(e) any person to whom they consider it appropriate to send a copy.

(9) The authority shall review the statement under section 172(5) in light of the report and any other information or advice which it considers relevant, shall make written recommendations as to the matters referred to in regulation 15(8)(a) and (b), and shall prepare a transition plan.

(10) The authority shall within one week of completing the review under section 172(5) send copies of the recommendations and the transition plan referred to in paragraph (9) to the persons referred to in paragraph (8).

Review of statement where child does not attend school

17.–(1) This regulation applies where an authority review a statement under section 172(5) other than on the making of an assessment and the child concerned does not attend a school.

(2) The authority shall prepare a report addressing the matters referred to in regulation 15(4), including the matters referred to in regulation 15(4)(e) in any case where the review referred to in paragraph (1) is commenced after the child has attained the age of 14 years or older, and for that purpose shall seek advice on those matters from the child's parent and any other person whose advice they consider appropriate in the case in question for the purpose of arriving at a satisfactory report.

(3) The authority shall invite the following persons to attend a meeting to be held on a date before the review referred to in paragraph (1) is required to be completed–

(a) the child's parent;

(b) where the review referred to in paragraph (1) is the first review commenced after the child has attained the age of 14 years, a representative of the social services authority;

(c) where subparagraph (b) applies, a person providing careers services under sections 8 to 10 of the Employment and Training Act 1973; and

(d) any person or persons whose attendance the authority consider appropriate.

(4) The authority shall not later than two weeks before the date on which the meeting referred to in paragraph (3) is to be held send to all the persons invited to that meeting a copy of the report which they propose to make under paragraph (2) and by written notice accompanying the copies shall request the recipients to submit to the authority written comments on the report and any other advice which they think appropriate.

(5) A representative of the authority shall attend the meeting.

(6) The meeting shall consider the matters referred to in regulation 15(7), including in any case where the review is commenced after the child has attained the age of 14 years the matters referred to in regulation 15(4)(e), and shall make

recommendations in accordance with regulation 15(8) and (9), including in any case where the child has attained the age of 14 years or older as aforesaid recommendations as to the matters referred to in regulation 15(8)(c).

(7) The report prepared by the authority under paragraph (2) shall be completed after the meeting referred to in paragraph (3) is held, shall contain the authority's assessment of the matters required to be considered by the meeting and their recommendations as to the matters required to be recommended by it, and shall refer to any difference between their assessment and recommendations and those of the meeting.

(8) The authority shall within one week of the date on which the meeting referred to in paragraph (3) was held send copies of the report completed under paragraph (7) to –

(a) the child's parent;

(b) the persons from whom they sought advice under paragraph (2);

(c) the persons who were invited to attend the meeting under paragraph (3); and

(d) any person to whom they consider it appropriate to send a copy.

(9) The authority shall review the statement under section 172(5) in light of the report and any other information or advice which it considers relevant, shall make written recommendations as to the matters referred to in regulation 15(8)(a) and (b), in any case where the review is the first review commenced after the child has attained the age of 14 years prepare a transition plan, and in any case where a transition plan exists amend the plan as they consider appropriate.

(10) The authority shall within one week of completing the review under section 172(5) send copies of the recommendations and any transition plan referred to in paragraph (9) to the persons referred to in paragraph (8).

Transfer of statements

18.–(1) This regulation applies where a child in respect of whom a statement is maintained moves from the area of the authority which maintains the statement ('the old authority') into that of another ('the new authority').

(2) The old authority shall transfer the statement to the new authority, and from the date of the transfer –

(a) the statement shall be treated for the purposes of the new authority's duties and functions under Part III of the Act and these Regulations as if it had been made by the new authority on the date on which it was made by the old authority, and

(b) where the new authority make an assessment under section 167 and the old authority have supplied the new authority with advice obtained in pursuance of a previous assessment regulation 6(5) shall apply as if the new authority had obtained the advice on the date on which the old authority obtained it.

(3) The new authority shall within 6 weeks of the date of the transfer serve a notice on the child's parent informing him –

(a) that the statement has been transferred,

(b) whether they propose to make an assessment under section 167, and

(c) when they propose to review the statement in accordance with paragraph (4).

(4) The new authority shall review the statement under section 172(5) before the expiry of whichever of the following two periods expires later –

(a) the period of twelve months beginning with the making of the statement, or as the case may be, with the previous review, or

(b) the period of three months beginning with the date of the transfer.

(5) Where by virtue of the transfer the new authority come under a duty to arrange the child's attendance at a school specified in the statement but in light of the child's move that attendance is no longer practicable the new authority may arrange for the child's attendance at another school appropriate for the child until such time as it is possible to amend the statement in accordance with paragraph 10 of Schedule 10 to the Act.

Restriction on disclosure of statements

19.–(1) Subject to the provisions of the Act and of these Regulations, a statement in respect of a child shall not be disclosed without the parent's consent except –

(a) to persons to whom, in the opinion of the authority concerned, the statement should be disclosed in the interests of the child;

(b) for the purposes of any appeal under the Act;

(c) for the purposes of educational research which, in the opinion of the authority, may advance the education of children with special educational needs, if, but only if, the person engaged in that research undertakes not to publish anything contained in, or derived from, a statement otherwise than in a form which does not identify any individual concerned including, in particular, the child concerned and his parent;

(d) on the order of any court or for the purposes of any criminal proceedings;

(e) for the purposes of any investigation under Part III of the Local Government Act 1974 (investigation of maladministration)(**j**);

(f) to the Secretary of State when he requests such disclosure for the purposes of deciding whether to give directions or make an order under section 68 or 99 of the Education Act 1944(**k**);

(g) for the purposes of an assessment of the needs of the child with respect to the provision of any statutory services for him being carried out by officers of a social services authority by virtue of arrangements made under section 5(5) of the Disabled Persons (Services, Consultation and Representation) Act 1986(**l**);

(h) for the purposes of a local authority in the performance of their duties under sections 22(3)(a), 85(4)(a), 86(3)(a) and 87(3) of the Children Act 1989(**m**); or

(i) to one of Her Majesty's Inspectors of Schools, or to a registered inspector or a member of an inspection team, who requests the right to inspect or take copies of a statement in accordance with section 3(3) of or paragraph 7 of Schedule 2 to the Education (Schools) Act 1992(**n**) respectively.

(2) The arrangements for keeping such statements shall be such as to ensure, so far as is reasonably practicable, that unauthorised persons do not have access to them.

(3) In this regulation any reference to a statement includes a reference to any representations, evidence, advice or information which is set out in the appendices to a statement.

(j) 1974 c.7; Part III has been amended by paragraph 9(1) of Schedule 10 to the Community Land Act 1975 (c.77), by paragraph 14 of Schedule 22 and Part XI of Schedule 34 to the Local Government, Planning and Land Act 1980 (c. 65), by paragraph 51(a) of Schedule 14 to the Local Government Act 1985 (c.51), by paragraph 4 of Schedule 3 to the Local Government Act 1988 (c.9), by paragraph 19 of Schedule 17 to the Housing Act 1988 (c.50), by sections 23(1), 25, 194(1) and (4), and 195(2) of, and paragraph 38 of Schedule 11 and Part II of Schedule 12 to, the Local Government and Housing Act 1989 (c.42), by section 1(6) of and paragraph 12 of Schedule 1 and paragraph 3 of Schedule 26 to the Water Act 1989 (c.15), and by section 2(1) of and paragraph 25 of Schedule 1 to the Water Consolidation (Consequential Provisions) Act 1991(c.60).

(k) 1944 c.31.

(l) 1986 c.33.

(m) 1989 c.41.

(n) 1992 c.38; paragraph 7 of Schedule 2 was amended by the Education Act 1993 (c.35), Schedule 19 paragraph 173(4).

PART IV

REVOCATION AND TRANSITIONAL PROVISIONS

Revocation of the 1983 Regulations

20.   Subject to regulation 21, the 1983 Regulations, the Education (Special Educational Needs)(Amendment) Regulations 1988(**o**) and the Education (Special Educational Needs)(Amendment) Regulations 1990(**p**) are hereby revoked.

Transitional provisions

21.–(1)   Subject to the following provisions of this regulation references in these Regulations to anything done under the Act or these Regulations shall be read in relation to the times, circumstances or purposes in relation to which a corresponding provision of the 1981 Act or the 1983 Regulations had effect and so far as the nature of the reference permits as including a reference to that corresponding provision.

(2)   Regulations 3 to 8 of the 1983 Regulations shall continue to apply in relation to any assessment where before 1st September 1994 in pursuance of section 5(5) of the 1981 Act the authority notify the parent that they have decided to make an assessment, and Part II of these Regulations shall not apply in relation to any such assessment.

(3)   Where regulations 3 to 8 of the 1983 Regulations continue to apply in relation to any assessment but the authority have not before 1st January 1995 –

(a)   notified the parent of their decision that they are not required to determine the special educational provision of the child in accordance with section 5(7) of the 1981 Act, or

(b)   served on the parent a copy of a proposed statement in accordance with section 7(3) of the 1981 Act

Part II of these Regulations shall apply in relation to the assessment from 1st January 1995 as if on that date the authority had given notice to the parent under section 167(4) of their decision to make an assessment.

(4)   Where in accordance with paragraph (3) above Part II of these Regulations applies in relation to an assessment the authority shall obtain advice in accordance with Part II, but advice obtained in accordance with the 1983 Regulations shall be considered to have been obtained under Part II if such advice is appropriate for the purpose of arriving at a satisfactory assessment under that Part.

(o)   S.I. 1988/1067.

(p)   S.I. 1990/1524.

(5)   Where before 1st September 1994 in accordance with section 5(3) of the 1981 Act the authority have served notice on the child's parent that they propose to make an assessment but they have not before that date notified the parent under section 5(5) of the 1981 Act that they have decided to make the assessment or notified them that they have decided not to make the assessment, the authority shall decide whether or not to make the assessment in accordance with section 167 and not later than 13th October 1994 give notice to the child's parent –

(a)   under section 167(4) of their decision to make an assessment, and of their reasons for making that decision, or

(b)   under section 167(6) of their decision not to assess the educational needs of the child,

and Part II of these Regulations shall apply to any such assessment.

(6)   Where before 1st September 1994 in accordance with section 9 of the 1981 Act a parent has asked the authority to arrange for an assessment to be made of the child's educational needs but the authority have not before that date notified the parent under section 5(5) of the 1981 Act that they have decided to make the assessment or notified them that they have decided not to make the assessment, the authority shall decide whether or not to make to make the assessment in accordance with section 167 and not later than 13th October 1994 give notice to the child's parent –

(a)   under section 167(4) of their decision to make an assessment, or

(b)   under section 172(3)(a) or 173(2)(a) of their decision not to comply with the request and of the parent's right to appeal to the Tribunal against the determination,

and Part II of these Regulations shall apply to any such assessment.

(7)   Regulation 10 of the 1983 Regulations shall continue to apply to the making of any statement where before 1st January 1995 the authority have served on the parent a copy of a proposed statement in accordance with section 7(3) of the 1981 Act, and regulations 12, 13 and 14(1) to (4) of these Regulations shall not apply to the making of any such statement.

(8)   Regulation 14(6) and (7) shall not apply in relation to a proposal to amend or cease to maintain a statement where an authority serve a notice under paragraph 6 of Schedule 1 to the 1981 Act(**q**) before 1st September 1994.

(9)   Regulations 15 to 17 shall not apply to any review of a statement which is required to be completed before 1st December 1994.

---

q)   Paragraph 6(4) of Schedule 1 was added by the Education Reform Act 1988 (c.40), Schedule 12, paragraph 85.

(10) Regulations 15 to 17 shall apply to a review of a statement which is not required to be completed before 1st December 1994, but where the statement was made under the 1981 Act they shall apply with any necessary modifications, including the following:

(a) where the review is the first review commenced after 1st September 1994 –

(i) the authority shall seek advice as to the objectives which the special educational provision for the child should meet rather than as to the child's progress towards meeting the objectives specified in the statement;

(ii) the authority shall seek advice as to the targets which should be established in furtherance of those objectives rather than as to the child's progress towards attaining any such targets;

(iii) where the child has attained the age of 14 years before the date on which the review is commenced the authority shall in any event seek advice as to any matters which are the appropriate subject of a transition plan;

(iv) the meeting held in accordance with regulation 15(7), 16(6) or 17(6) shall consider the matters referred to in those regulations as modified by subparagraphs (i) to (iii) above as appropriate, and shall make recommendations under regulation 15(8), 16(7) or 17(7) but including recommendations as to the objectives referred to in subparagraph (i), the targets referred to in subparagraph (ii) and where appropriate the transition plan referred to in paragraph (iii); and

(v) the authority shall review the statement in accordance with regulation 15(12), 16(9) or 17(9), shall make recommendations as to the matters referred to in those regulations read in light of the modifications in this subparagraph, shall prepare a transition plan where subparagraph (iii) above applies, and shall in any event specify the objectives referred to in subparagraph (i) above;

and

(b) where the review is not the first review commenced after 1st September 1994 any reference to objectives shall include a reference to objectives specified in accordance with subparagraph (a)(v) above in addition to objectives specified in a statement.

(11) Subject to paragraphs (12) and (13), regulation 12 of the 1983 Regulations shall continue to apply in relation to a transfer on a date before 1st September 1994, and regulation 18 of these Regulations shall not apply in relation to such a transfer.

(12) Notwithstanding paragraph (11), where a statement has been transferred on a date before 1st September 1994 and the new authority has not before that date either —

(a) in pursuance of section 5(3) of the 1981 Act served a notice on the child's parent that they propose to make an assessment, or

(b) in pursuance of regulation 12(4) of the 1983 Regulations notified the child's parent that they do not propose to make an assessment,

they shall comply with regulation 18(3) of these Regulations before 13th October 1994.

(13) Notwithstanding paragraph (11), where a statement has been transferred on a date before 1st September 1994 the new authority shall review the statement under section 172(5) before the expiry of whichever of the following two periods expires later —

(a) the period of twelve months beginning with the making of the statement, or as the case may be, with the previous review, or

(b) the period ending on 30th November 1994.

(14) Regulation 11 of the 1983 Regulations shall not apply to statements made before or after 1st September 1994 and regulation 19 of these Regulations shall apply, except that a statement may be disclosed for the purposes of any appeal under section 8 of the 1981 Act(r) as well as for the purposes of any appeal under the Act.

(r)   Section 8(1) was substituted by the Education Reform Act 1988 (c.40), Schedule 12, paragraph 84.

SCHEDULE

PART A

NOTICE TO PARENT

To: [*name and address of parent*]

1. Accompanying this notice is a copy of a statement of the special educational needs of [**name of child**] which [**name of authority**] ('the authority') propose to make under the Education Act 1993.

2. You may express a preference for the maintained, grant maintained or grant-maintained special school you wish your child to attend and may give reasons for your preference.

3. If you wish to express such a preference you must do so not later than 15 days from the date on which you receive this notice and the copy of the statement or 15 days from the date on which you last attend a meeting in accordance with paragraph 10 or 11 below, whichever is later. If the 15th day falls on a weekend or a bank holiday you must do so not later than the following working day.

4. If you express a preference in accordance with paragraphs 2 and 3 above the authority are required to specify the name of the school you prefer in the statement, and accordingly to arrange special educational provision at that school, unless –

   (a) the school is unsuitable to your child's age, ability or aptitude or to his/her special educational needs, or

   (b) the attendance of your child at the school would be incompatible with the provision of efficient education for the children with whom he/she would be educated or the efficient use of resources.

5. The authority will normally arrange special educational provision in a maintained, grant-maintained or grant-maintained special school. However, if you believe that the authority should arrange special educational provision for your child at a non-maintained special school or an independent school you may make representations to that effect.

6. The following maintained, grant-maintained and grant-maintained special schools provide [**primary/secondary**] education in the area of the authority:

   [**Here list all maintained, grant-maintained, and grant-maintained special schools in the authority's area which provide primary education, or list all such schools which provide secondary education, depending on whether the child requires primary or secondary education. Alternatively, list the required information in a list attached to this notice.**]

7. A list of the non-maintained special schools which make special educational provision for pupils with special educational needs in England and Wales and are approved by the Secretary of State for Education or the Secretary of State for Wales is attached to this notice.

8. A list of the independent schools in England and Wales which are approved by the Secretary of State for Education or the Secretary of State for Wales as suitable for the admission of children for whom statements of special educational needs are maintained is attached to this notice.

9. You are entitled to make representations to the authority about the content of the statement. If you wish to make such representations you must do so not later than 15 days from the date on which you receive this notice, or 15 days from the date on which you last attended a meeting in accordance with the next paragraph, whichever is the later date.

10. You are entitled, not later than 15 days from the date on which you receive this notice, to require the authority to arrange a meeting between you and an officer of the authority at which any part of the statement, or all of it, may be discussed. In particular, any advice on which the statement is based may be discussed.

11. If having attended a meeting in accordance with paragraph 10 above you still disagree with any part of the assessment in question, you may within 15 days of the date of the meeting require the authority to arrange a meeting or meetings to discuss the advice which they consider relevant to the part of the assessment you disagree with. They will arrange for the person who gave the advice, or some other person whom they think appropriate, to attend the meeting.

12. If at the conclusion of the procedure referred to above the authority serve on you a statement with which you disagree you may appeal to the Special Educational Needs Tribunal against the description of your child's special educational needs, against the special educational provision specified including the school named, or, if no school is named, against that fact.

13. All correspondence with the authority should be addressed to the officer responsible for this case:

   [Here set out name, address and telephone number of case officer, and any reference number which should be quoted.]

_____   _____

[Date]   [Signature of officer responsible]

PART B
STATEMENT OF SPECIAL EDUCATIONAL NEEDS

Part 1: Introduction

1. In accordance with section 168 of the Education Act 1993 ('the Act') and the Education (Special Educational Needs) Regulations 1994 ('the Regulations'), the following statement is made by [*here set out name of authority*]('the authority') in respect of the child whose name and other particulars are mentioned below.

Child

Surname ....   Other names ....

Home address ....

....   Sex ....

....   Religion ....

Date of Birth ....   Home language ....

Child's parent or person responsible

Surname ....   Other names ....

Home address ....

....   Relationship to child ....

....

Telephone No. ....

---

2. When assessing the child's special educational needs the authority took into consideration, in accordance with regulation 10 of the Regulations, the representations, evidence and advice set out in the Appendices to this statement.

PART 2: SPECIAL EDUCATIONAL NEEDS

[Here set out the child's special educational needs, in terms of the child's learning difficulties which call for special educational provision, as assessed by the authority.]

PART 3: SPECIAL EDUCATIONAL PROVISION

Objectives

[Here specify the objectives which the special educational provision for the child should aim to meet.]

Educational provision to meet needs and objectives

[Here specify the special educational provision which the authority consider appropriate to meet the needs specified in Part 2 and to meet the objectives specified in this Part, and in particular specify —

(a)   any appropriate facilities and equipment, staffing arrangements and curriculum,

(b)   any appropriate modifications to the application of the National Curriculum,

(c)   any appropriate exclusions from the application of the National Curriculum, in detail, and the provision which it is proposed to substitute for any such exclusions in order to maintain a balanced and broadly based curriculum; and

(d)   where residential accommodation is appropriate, that fact].

Monitoring

[Here specify the arrangements to be made for —

(a)   regularly monitoring progress in meeting the objectives specified in this Part,

(b)   establishing targets in furtherance of those objectives,

(c)   regularly monitoring the targets referred to in (b),

(d)   regularly monitoring the appropriateness of any modifications to the application of the National Curriculum, and

(e)   regularly monitoring the appropriateness of any provision substituted for exclusions from the application of the National Curriculum.

Here also specify any special arrangements for reviewing this statement.]

PART 4: PLACEMENT

[Here specify —

(a)   the type of school which the authority consider appropriate for the child and the name of the school for which the parent has expressed a preference or, where the authority are required to specify the name of a school, the name of the school which they consider would be appropriate for the child and should be specified, or

(b)   the provision for his education otherwise than at a school which the authority consider appropriate.]

PART 5: NON-EDUCATIONAL NEEDS

[Here specify the non-educational needs of the child for which the authority consider provision is appropriate if the child is to properly benefit from the special educational provision specified in Part 3.]

PART 6: NON-EDUCATIONAL PROVISION

[Here specify any non-educational provision which the authority propose to make available or which they are satisfied will be made available by a district health authority, a social services authority or some other body, including the arrangements for its provision. Also specify the objectives of the provision, and the arrangements for monitoring progress in meeting those objectives.]

_____   _____

Date   *A duly authorised officer of the authority*

Appendix A: Parental Representations

[Here set out any written representations made by the parent of the child under section 167(1)(d) of or paragraph 4(1) of Schedule 10 to the Act and a summary which the parent has accepted as accurate of any oral representations so made or record that no such representations were made.]

Appendix B: Parental Evidence

[Here set out any written evidence either submitted by the parent of the child under section 167(1)(d) of the Act or record that no such evidence was submitted.]

Appendix C: Advice from the Child's Parent

[Here set out the advice obtained under regulation 6(1)(a).]

Appendix D: Educational Advice

[Here set out the advice obtained under regulation 6(1)(b).]

Appendix E: Medical Advice

[Here set out the advice obtained under regulation 6(1)(c).]

Appendix F: Psychological Advice

[Here set out the advice obtained under regulation 6(1)(d).]

Appendix G: Advice from the Social Services Authority

[Here set out the advice obtained under regulation 6(1)(e).]

Appendix H: Other Advice Obtained by the Authority

[Here set out the advice obtained under regulation 6(1)(f).]

6th April 1994

Date

Eric Forth

Parliamentary Under Secretary of State, Department for Education

7th April 1994

Date

John Redwood

Secretary of State for Wales

EXPLANATORY NOTE

(This Note is not part of the Regulations)

These Regulations relate to the assessment of special educational needs and to statements of such needs under Part III of the Education Act 1993. Part III replaces with modifications the provisions relating to such assessments and statements in the Education Act 1981, and these Regulations replace with modifications the Education (Special Educational Needs) Regulations 1983, which are revoked (regulation 20).

The Regulations make provision for a head teacher to delegate his functions under them generally to a qualified teacher, or in a particular case to the staff member who teaches the child (regulation 3).

The Regulations provide that local education authorities in making an assessment of a child's special educational needs must seek advice from the child's parent, educational advice, medical advice, psychological advice, advice from the social services authority and any other advice which they consider appropriate for the purpose of arriving at a satisfactory assessment (regulation 6). If such advice has been obtained on making a previous assessment within the last 12 months and certain persons are satisfied that it is sufficient, it is not necessary to obtain new advice (regulation 6(5)). Detailed provision is made as to the persons from whom educational, medical and psychological advice must be sought (regulations 7 to 9). It is provided that in making an assessment an authority shall take into consideration representations from the parent, evidence submitted by the parent, and the advice which has been obtained (regulation 10).

The Regulations prescribe the form and content of a notice to be served on a parent with a draft statement of special educational needs, and of a statement of special educational needs (regulations 12 and 13 and Part A and B of the Schedule respectively).

The Regulations also supplement the procedural framework for making an assessment and a statement contained in Part III of the Education Act 1993 and Schedules 9 and 10 thereto. Detailed provision is made for the service of documents by post (regulation 4). They require copies of notices of a local education authority's proposal to make an assessment, their decision to make an assessment or notices of a parent's request for an assessment to be made, to be served on the social services authority, the district health authority and the head teacher of the child's school (regulation 5). Subject to exceptions, they require local education authorities to carry out various steps in making an assessment or a statement within prescribed time limits (regulations 11 and 14 respectively).

Detailed provision is made as to how a review of a statement by a local education authority under section 172 of the Education Act 1993 is to be carried out (regulations 15 to 17). In particular it is provided that where a child attends school where the review is the first review after he has attained the age of 14 the head teacher of his school will obtain advice, the local education authority will chair a meeting, and the authority will prepare a transition plan (regulation 16). In the case of any other review where a child attends school the head teacher of his school will obtain advice, he will chair a meeting and report to the local education authority (regulation 15). Where a child does not attend school provision is made for the local authority to obtain advice, to chair a meeting, and where the review is the first after he attains the age of 14, to prepare a transition plan (regulation 17).

The Regulations provide for the transfer of a statement from one local education authority to another (regulation 18). The duties of the transferor are transferred to the transferee, and within six weeks of the transfer the transferee must serve a notice on the parent informing him of the transfer, whether they propose to make an assessment, and when they propose to review the statement (regulation 18(2) and (3)). It is provided that where it would not be practicable to require the transferee to arrange for the child's attendance at a school specified in the statement they need not do so, but can arrange for attendance at another school until it is possible to amend the statement (regulation 18(5)).

There are restrictions on the disclosure of statements and steps are to be taken to avoid unauthorised persons having access to them (regulation 19).

Detailed provision is made for the transition from the regime imposed by the 1983 Regulations to the regime imposed by these Regulations (regulation 21). In particular if an assessment has been commenced before 1st September 1994 the local education authority may continue to make the assessment under the 1983 Regulations, and may make any statement following the assessment under them as well (regulation 21(2) and (7)). These Regulations, and the time limits they impose, will not apply. However if the assessment is not complete before 1st January 1995 these Regulations will apply to the assessment as if it had been commenced under them on that date (regulation 21(3)).